THE BOOK OF
FIRST
CORINTHIANS

Paul A. Hamar

THE BOOK OF FIRST CORINTHIANS

Gospel Publishing House
Springfield, Missouri
02-0316

In Dedication:
To my late father, who was pastor, teacher, and example;
To my mother who has prayed much for me;
To my wife who has supported me in every way;
To the Rev. Dick Dron and Professor Dwayne Turner
who encouraged me to proceed in this work.

2nd Printing 1994

Library of Congress Cataloging in Publication Data

Hamar, Paul A. 1949—
  The Book of First Corinthians.

  (The Radiant commentary on the New Testament)
  Bibliography: p
  Includes index.
  1. Bible. N.T. 1 Corinthians—Commentaries.
  I. Bible. N.T. 1 Corinthians. English. 1980.
  II. Title. III. Series: Radiant commentary on the New Testament.
  BS 2675.3.H27   227'.207   80-16358
  ISBN 0-88243-316-4

Printed in the United States of America

Abbreviations

All Scripture quotations are from the King James Version, unless specified otherwise. Other versions used herein may be identified by the following codes:

ASV   *The American Standard Version.* Nashville: Thomas Nelson, Inc., 1901.

GNT   *The Greek New Testament* (Kurt Aland, *et al*). New York: American Bible Society, 1966.

NASB   *The New American Standard Bible.* Carol Stream, IL: Creation House, Inc., 1973.

NEB   *The New English Bible.* Fair Lawn, NJ: Oxford University Press, Inc., 1961.

NIV   *The New International Version.* Grand Rapids: Zondervan Publishing House, 1978.

RSV   *The Revised Standard Version.* Nashville: Thomas Nelson, Inc., 1971.

TEV   *Today's English Version (Good News for Modern Man).* New York: American Bible Society, 1971.

Amp   *The Amplified Bible.* Grand Rapids: Zondervan Publishing House, 1965.

Conf   *Confraternity Edition of the Holy Bible.* Washington, D.C.: Confraternity of Christian Doctrine.

Gspd   *The New Testament: An American Translation* (Edgar J. Goodspeed). Chicago: University of Chicago, 1923, 1948.

Mof   *The New Testament, A New Translation* (James Moffatt). New York: Harper & Row, Publishers, 1964.

Phi   *The New Testament in Modern English* (J. B. Phillips). New York: The Macmillan Company, 1958.

Tay   *The Living Bible, Paraphrased* (Kenneth N. Taylor). Wheaton, IL: Tyndale House Publishers, 1971.

Contents

Author's Foreword   9

    I   The Epistle's Introduction (1:1-9)   17

   II   Division and Unity (1:10 to 4:21)   21

  III   Indifference in Social
                Morality (5:1 to 6:20)   43

  IV   Marriage and Celibacy (7:1-40)   55

   V   Liberty and Love (8:1 to 11:1)   71

  VI   Public Worship (11:2 to 14:40)   93

 VII   The Resurrection (15:1-58)   137

VIII   General Instructions and
               Greetings (16:1-24)   161

Notes   173

Bibliography   183

Index   185

Author's
Foreword

A. The History, Geography, and Character of Corinth

It is necessary at the very outset to briefly summarize the history of this important city. It was an aggressive, colonizing city in 800-700 B.C., with Corinthian bronze and pottery being proverbial. In 146 B.C., the city was burned by the Roman Mummius, as the Achaean League made a last desperate, but unsuccessful, stand against the Roman Empire.

In 46 B.C., it was refounded by Julius Caesar under the name of *Colonia Julia Corinthus* (or *Laus Julii Corinthus*). Corinth soon became the most important city in Greece, and the capital of the Roman province of Achaia.

Eventually the city's position declined, but it remained until 1858, when the old city was destroyed. Soon after, a new city was built 3½ miles away; it remains today.

The geography of Corinth played an important part in its rise and power. Corinth was located on the Isthmus of Greece about 50 miles west of Athens. This isthmus connected the Peloponnesus with the Greek mainland and separated the Ionian Sea from the Aegean.

To the south was the Acro-corinthus (1985 feet high) and the Oneion range of mountains. Corinth itself looked down on the Saronic and Corinthian gulfs, which furnished the main artery of commerce between the Aegean and Euxine (Black) Seas, and the western Mediterranean. To the west was the port of Lechaeum (1½ miles away), linked to Corinth by double walls; the eastern port was Cenchreae (8½ miles away). A shipway connected the two harbors; thus, it was called the "city of the two seas."

Across this isthmus was transported a major share of trade

goods. It was preferred rather than the long, risky voyage around the stormy, rocky cape of Malea, to the south of the Peloponnesus. Large ships meant transshipping the cargo; smaller vessels were hauled across the isthmus on a sort of tramway with wooden tracks. This trip saved 200 miles.

Nero attempted to build a canal across this isthmus, but failed. The present canal was dug during the years 1881-1893, and followed the course Nero had suggested.

The city of Corinth had a mixed population. It was the first city in Greece to admit gladiatorial games, which suggests the Roman influence. But the population, while originally consisting largely of Roman freedmen, grew to include many native Greeks as well as foreigners. In fact, there is evidence that by the time Paul arrived in Corinth it had become largely Hellenized. There were Jews and at least one synagogue. And it has been estimated that 50 percent or more of the population were slaves.

This city, with 400,000 to 600,000, was surpassed in total population only by Rome, Alexandria, and Antioch. But the population was a medley of races who had seemingly retained the worst of each original strain. It was a "renowned and voluptuous city, where the vices of East and West met (Henry H. Halley, *Halley's Bible Handbook* [Grand Rapids: Zondervan Publishing House, 1965], p. 593). It was a city where "Greeks, Latins, Syrians, Asiatics, Egyptians and Jews, bought and sold, labored and revelled, quarrelled and hobnobbed, in the city and its ports, as nowhere else in Greece (Leon Morris, *Tyndale New Testament Commentaries*, Vol. 7 [Grand Rapids: Wm. B. Eerdmans Publishing Co., 1958], pp. 15, 16). Someone once called it "the Vanity Fair of the Roman Empire."

It was a city of much cultural advancement and prided itself on this. It had many studios, workshops, and schools of philosophy. Dominating the center of the city was the *agora* or marketplace. Archaeologists have found shops facing the marketplace which were supplied with fresh, cold water through subterranean channels connected to a well. It is also interesting to note that, in accordance with 1 Corinthians 10:25, one shop was called *macellum* or shambles.

Corinth was a city of much corruption. A glance at the expressions of the day will support this. To use the phrase "Corinthian words" indicated pretensions in philosophy and letters. "To Corinthianize" was polite Greek for "go to the devil." "To live as a Corinthian" meant luxury and licentiousness, and the phrases "Corinthian banquet" and "Corinthian drinkers" were similarly proverbial. The ideal of the Corinthian was the personal and selfish development of the individual. The merchant who cheated and lied, but gained his objective; the hedonist who surrounded himself with every lust and pleasure; the athlete who took haughty pride in his body—these men were honored in Corinthian society. True Corinthians were proud, undefeated, lawless men.

Corinth was also the center for much debased heathen worship. There were impure cults, such as those of the gods Serapis and Isis, and others from Egypt and Asia. Poseidon, the sea god under whose patronage the Isthmian games were held, was worshiped. Aphrodite's temple crowned the Acro-corinthus. Here a very debased worship evolved. More than 1,000 priestesses or prostitutes called *hieroduli* served the temple and brought their fees as offerings to the goddess.

All of this was important when Paul chose Corinth as a center for evangelism. But his choice was probably determined by the location of Corinth and the fact that he could expand from this center to much of the empire. The Book of Acts records Paul's work in Corinth.

B. Paul's Work in Corinth

After these things he departed from Athens, and came to Corinth. And he found a certain Jew named Aquila, a man of Pontus by race, lately come from Italy, with his wife Priscilla, because Claudius had commanded all the Jews to depart from Rome: and he came unto them; and because he was of the same trade, he abode with them, and they wrought; for by their trade they were tentmakers. And he reasoned in the synagogue every sabbath, and persuaded Jews and Greeks (Acts 18:1-4, *ASV*). (See also 1 Corinthians 2:1-5.)

After some time the Jews apparently rejected him and Paul quit preaching in the synagogue and went "unto the Gentiles" (Acts 18:6). He set up headquarters in the house of Justus (Titus Justus; his name suggests his Roman citizenship). It seems he used this house as his preaching base, but he didn't stop living

11

with Aquila and Priscilla. As has been noted by others, this was not the place to avoid trouble, but it was the perfect location for being found by the hungry God-fearer who had previously frequented the synagogue. A good number came to Christ, including Crispus, chief ruler of the synagogue. Many fine scholars, such as Holtzmann and Ramsay, believe this was the same Crispus referred to in 1 Corinthians 1:14. He was a Jew with a Latin name; according to tradition, he became the Bishop of Aegina (W. Robertson Nicoll, ed., *The Expositor's Greek New Testament*, Vol. 2 [Grand Rapids: Wm. B. Eerdmans Publishing Co., 1952]). Sosthenes then succeeded Crispus.

Trouble did come and a mob dragged Paul before Gallio, the Roman deputy and a brother to the philosopher Seneca. He rejected the arguments of the Jews, and the Greeks in anger took Sosthenes (who may be the one referred to in 1 Corinthians 1:1; it is questionable) and beat him in front of Gallio. Gallio may have allowed it because he considered it an act of justice or a sign of popular approval for his position (Charles R. Erdman, *The First Epistle of Paul to the Corinthians* [Philadelphia: Westminster Press, 1966]). Yet Luke records that he paid little or no attention. Certainly this action may be considered at least an unspoken sanction by the Roman government for Paul and the spread of the gospel in Greece.

Paul remained in Corinth for about 18 months, after which Apollos came to minister (Acts 18:24, 27, 28). Paul's teaching and preaching style may well have differed from Apollos' highly rhetorical style, but the message remained constant.

C. Paul's Continued Contact With Corinth

Paul probably came to Corinth around A.D. 50; assuming the conference at Jerusalem (Acts 15) took place in A.D. 49. According to an inscription at Delphi, Gallio took office in the summer of A.D. 51. Paul left Corinth not long after Gallio's arrival.

Paul continued to hear from Corinth. He evangelized in Asia until perhaps the spring of A.D. 56. The Feast of Pentecost was in A.D. 57. He left Asia from Ephesus (1 Corinthians 16:8) to attend this feast, possibly hastening because of the riots in Ephesus (Acts 19:21ff). Some have indicated that the Passover imagery in 1 Corinthians 5:7 suggests an Easter date for the writing of this letter, in A.D. 55 or 56, from Ephesus. This would have occurred then before Paul went to Troas during his third missionary journey.

Before a final approximation is made a few items must be further considered. Paul visited Corinth between A.D. 50 and 52. Perhaps he visited again in the 3 or 4 years that followed (2 Corinthians 2:1; 12:14, 20, 21; 13:2). After this may have followed the "lost" letter of 1 Corinthians 5:9, which apparently dealt with immorality. Some have suggested that part of this letter is preserved in 2 Corinthians 6:14 to 7:1. But this would not have to be the case since 1 Corinthians superseded the old letter. Perhaps, as some have suggested, the Corinthians misconstrued this in-between or "painful" visit (2 Corinthians 2:1; 12:20, 21) and defied Paul, resulting in the passage in 1 Corinthians 4:21. There is no mention in 1 Corinthians of a recent visit and no real time between the "lost" letter and 1 Corinthians. But 2 Corinthians 2:1; 12:14, 20, 21; and 13:2 suggest two visits before 2 Corinthians; thus, it may be there was a second visit before the "lost" or "previous" letter. After this came 1 Corinthians in A.D. 55 or 56.

D. The Occasion of the "First" Epistle to Corinth

It appears Paul wrote this Epistle because he received a letter from Corinth, brought to him by Stephanas, Fortunatus, and Achaicus (1 Corinthians 16:17). He also received reports of a disturbing nature from the household of Chloe (1 Corinthians 1:11) and from Apollos (16:12). These reports and letters pointed to some of the problems in the Corinthian church. Deplorable disunity was present; there was a problem with incest, a violation of the seventh commandment; there was a lack of concern for spiritually weaker brothers in Christ; there was a legal dispute being conducted in heathen courts by church members; some were dishonoring the Communion service; there was a lack of order in the public services; and there were some false ideas on the Resurrection.

This Epistle then has great importance, for it responds to these problems. It also reveals the personality and character of Paul and his methods in a heathen city. Further, it gives us at least a

13

partial glimpse into Paul's relationship to this church. The Corinthian church apparently was made up largely of Gentiles with no training in the Old Testament; their pagan background stood in opposition to Christian principles; there was a marked social bigotry and distinction (7:17-24; 11:21-34); some had been steeped in heathen vices which were not easily overthrown; they had no New Testament as we have; good teachers were not always around; and the Greeks were proud of both their factious spirit and their intellectualism, even though it had degenerated. Paul responds quickly and powerfully in this letter.

E. The Authenticity of 1 Corinthians

Some doubt the authenticity of this Epistle. Robertson and Plummer have responded: "Both the external and the internal evidence for the Pauline authorship are so strong that those who attempt to show that the apostle was not the writer succeed chiefly in proving their own incompetence as critics."

The external proof regarding this Epistle is strong. It was the first New Testament writing to be cited by name in Christian literature. It is mentioned by Clement (I Ep. 47), in the Epistle of Barnabas (4:9-11); by Hermas (Mand. 4:4); by Ignatius; by Polycarp, in *the Didache*; by Iraneus; by Tertullian (he quotes it more than 400 times); by Origen, Chrysostom, Theodoret, Oecumenius, Aquinas, and Clement of Alexandria (who quotes it more than 130 times); and it appears at the head of the Pauline epistles in the Muratorian Canon.

It did not take a leading part at first among the New Testament writings because it had little to say specifically on those things that chiefly interested the Ante-Nicene church. But in the fourth century, with the problems in Christian morals and discipline, it came to the forefront. It came to the front again during the Reformation (1496-1519).

The internal proof regarding this letter is equally strong and indisputable. It is interesting to note that of the 5,594 Greek words in the New Testament, this Epistle employs 963; 103 peculiar to itself, 68 classical, 22 of postclassical authors, one specifically Septuagint term, one Aramaic sentence, and 11 special words.

14

The text contains few conspicuous textual difficulties and has been carefully preserved. It fits in with the known situation at Corinth and coincides with the account in Acts. Further, Paul is mentioned in the salutations and elsewhere (1:12-17; 16:21). While the letter contains reproof, it was apparently accepted as genuine by the Corinthians.

In fact, until recent criticism by such men as Bauer, Loman, van Manen, and Steck, this Book was accepted as authentic by nearly everyone who examined it. Their arguments regarding interpolations, divisions, and contradictions are not worth discussion here. First Corinthians is an orderly Book that falls into a clear series of subjects, and there can be little doubt of its genuineness and testimony to this generation.

F. The Teaching of 1 Corinthians

The Book covers many themes. It discusses union with Christ and what disgraces, hallows, and consummates such a union. It discusses the Cross and its social implications. Doctrine covers every page. The doctrine of Jesus Christ is enlarged upon in numerous passages such as: 1:2, 3, 17-31; 2:2, 6-8, 14; 3:11, 16, 19; 6:19, 20; 8:6; 15:1-4; Romans 1:19-23. The Holy Spirit is discussed in such passages as: chapters 2, 12, and 14; 2:6 to 3:6; 6:11, 19, 20. Other doctrines covered are: the nature of the Christian community; the position of Christ's ministers (chapters 3 and 4); the Lord's Supper (chapter 11); and death and the Resurrection (chapter 15). At the very center of every discussion, however, is Christ—His presence, His lordship, and the redeeming power of the Cross.

According to this letter, it is possible to know many things and be able to glibly talk about them. But great care must be taken that everything is placed in the perspective of the work of Christ, so the spirit of the city does not invade the church and create excessive individualism. When that happens the church ceases to minister to itself, it becomes untrue to the central facts of its existence, and it fails to live up to what it should be and can be in the scheme and economy of God.

I

The Epistle's Introduction
(1:1-9)

A. The Salutation 1:1-3

This letter opens in the usual first-century way, listing the writer(s), those addressed, and a prayer. That this letter was written by the apostle Paul is beyond doubt. This is the Paul who once called himself a "Hebrew of the Hebrews" (Philippians 3:5), had the Damascus Road experience of Acts 9, wrote nearly half the books of the New Testament, and has been designated "the Apostle of the Gentiles." That he is an apostle, Paul makes clear in the very first verse. While suggesting his position and authority (apostle), he also notes its divine origin ("called") and its divine order ("will of God"). Here in the beginning Paul wants his readers to know that what he writes to them is from the Lord.

The co-writer of this letter is not so easily identified. Apparently he was a minister of lower rank, but nonetheless a fellow minister. It could be he was a Corinthian. Some have even suggested this is the Sosthenes mentioned in Acts 18:17. It is possible, but the name was so common that it is difficult to be certain.

When we read further in this letter and see the problems plaguing the Corinthians, we find it interesting that Paul calls them saints (v. 2). Yet it is the work of Christ that makes someone a saint, not the work of a body of men or the judgment of men. Sainthood is caused by the internal purification and reformation of the soul, as here suggested by the word *sanctified.*

We might conclude here that this letter was intended at least for more than just Corinth. The phrase "with all that in every place" would suggest that. Whether that intention was ever carried out is not known.

Shortly Paul will begin to discuss the problem of division at Corinth. But even here there is a veiled reference to that when Paul makes Christ Lord of everyone. True sanctification will produce genuine fellowship with other believers in Christ.

The greeting of grace and peace from both God the Father and God the Son was to become the typical Christian greeting. Especially is that true of Paul's writings.[1] The greeting covers God's gifts and blessings, and His attitude and desires toward those who love and serve Him.

B. The Thanksgiving (for Enrichment) (1:4-9)

Paul will say some difficult things before he has concluded this letter. Yet despite the problems, there is always something to thank the Lord for. And Paul wants the Corinthians to understand this. After all, these who had become Christians were a vast improvement over their heathen neighbors. The grace of God is an effective worker (v. 4), even though the change may seem more apparent in some than in others.

This grace is clearly of God; thus, the work done is of God also (v. 5). He had enriched these readers in a large way. Surprisingly, Paul notes their enrichment in two particular ways: in utterance or telling of truth, and in knowledge or the grasp of truth. Later, it will appear that he rebukes the readers for these very things. A careful reading, however, will lead us to understand that what Paul rebukes is the pride or the attitude in these things. With a proper attitude, knowledge and utterance can be a very powerful combination.

These readers heard the gospel, accepted it, and the consequence was their equality with other Christians. This "gift" (v. 7) may be salvation, good gifts in general, or a special equipment of the Holy Spirit. Whatever its precise reference, these so blessed are thus pointed to the second coming of Jesus Christ, when their use of these gifts shall be tested and they shall see the culmination of the work of the Spirit.

Until that day Christ will continue what He has begun; the work of confirming, sanctifying, or making perfect and unreprovable (v. 8). As *The Expositor's Greek Testament* suggests, He will confirm character as they have confirmed their testimony.[2]

18

And that confirmation will continue because God is faithful. Phillips' translation puts it nicely when it reads: "God is utterly dependable . . ." (v. 9). It is this God who called us to fellowship with His Son Jesus[3] and it is He who will finish the beautiful work He has begun. After all, Jesus Christ, under the direction of the Father, is both the "Author and Finisher" of our faith.

II

Division
and
Unity
(1:10 to 4:21)

A. Exhortation to Unity (1:10-17)

After his very positive opening remarks, however, it does not take Paul long to begin to correct the difficulties at Corinth that had come to his attention. "Now" (v. 10) contrasts what follows with what has preceded. He appeals to them with great solemnity, yet great gentleness, to be united together under Christ. Some might argue that it is very difficult to be so united because of differences in background, personality, and approach. But when Paul urges them to "speak the same thing" and be in unity, he is referring to unity in love, doctrine, and purpose which is both essential and mandatory. In fact, "speak the same thing" is a classical expression used of political communities that were free from factions, or of different states that entertained friendly relations with each other. Paul wishes his readers to be restored to a rightful condition of love in Christ, and if there cannot be a unity of choice, at least maintain a unity of feeling and affection.

Lest the Corinthians deny the difficulties, Paul records his source of information. The reports had come from "the house of Chloe" (v. 11). The reports were true beyond any reasonable doubt. So Paul tells them precisely what they have been doing and saying. Indeed it seems four major divisions had developed: One followed Paul, whom we are familiar with already; one followed Apollos, who differed not in message but apparently in method, having a more rhetorical, eloquent style; one group followed Cephas or Peter, the "hero" of Pentecost (these were probably conservative Jewish-Christians); and one group said they followed Christ (these may have been ultraconservative followers, or individuals with an ego problem). Whatever the supports on which these groups rested, Paul quickly brings them to ground with three short questions (v. 13). These questions suggest the unity, work, and supremacy of Christ, and Paul intends a negative answer to each question. Christ is not divided; He died for all; He is Lord of all. In the Spirit of Christ, such division is the heart of folly itself.

There is one Body and Paul makes it clear, when he uses those who followed him as examples, that it must remain one church under Jesus Christ. In fact, Paul notes his thanks that he had not baptized many at Corinth, in water, and that he had especially not baptized in his own name.[4]

We catch a glimpse of the ministry of Paul. He had probably baptized Crispus and Gaius because they were early converts to Christ. However, Paul's primary task was not sacraments, but preaching. There were others, perhaps even deacons, to baptize. Paul preferred to preach, not in his own wisdom or ability, but in the power of the Holy Spirit; the cross of Christ being the center of his message. With these words, then, Paul not only tells his readers where his union exists, but also prepares us for the next section.

B. The Expression of God's Wisdom and Power (1:18-25)

Paul wishes to turn the minds of his readers to the source of our union and unity—the Cross. He does so by displaying it as the greatest expression of wisdom and power the world has ever seen. To some it does not appear that way; it appears foolish. Paul speaks in irony for it seems foolish merely because the message is simple and the listeners are blind, proud, and mocking. These who are perishing[5] stubbornly take their own way and consider the Cross foolish. But it is this consideration that is causing them to perish. They mock their only hope. And the fact of their perishing proves the fallacy of their thinking.

But to those who are being saved[6] this Cross is the very expression of God's power. Notice that Paul includes himself ("us," v. 18) in those who are heirs of salvation. It is not glory in himself, but in the cross of Christ. The range of God's power covers not only the material realm of controlling the universe, and not only the mental realm of changing men's opinions, particularly at salvation; but also the realm of the moral and spiritual. By the Cross we are united with Christ, cleansed and purified, and "kept" unto salvation.

At the same time (v. 19) we are told of God's view of man's wisdom. Isaiah 29:14 is quoted with slight alterations. God rendered useless the imagined wisdom of Jerusalem, and as it happened then so it will happen again. The very highest "earthly" wisdom and understanding shall be as nonsense. And the fact is no man can dispute God on the matter. The world and God are at variance. Each considers the other one foolish. But God has made the world's imagined wisdom foolish, which cannot be said for the world in return. Paul establishes this by three questions: Question one establishes that where the Cross is preached human wisdom cannot stand. Paul does not say there are no worldly-wise men left. In question two the scribe may be alongside because human wisdom may refer to or use Holy Writ. But a knowledge of the Word without submission to it only creates helplessness and chaos. Again, in question three, the "disputer" may indicate one who understands his own "times"; but that is not enough. Question four is really only a summation and answer to the other three questions.

In point of fact, God deliberately chose a way that would confound man's wisdom and reason. Man in his wisdom could not discover what God is like. He has never discovered his duty to God without revelation. And that is part of God's wise providence. Rather, God chose deliberately the "foolishness of preaching." It is possible that Paul is referring to content. Nonetheless, God's work was considered foolish because the world would not give up its "wisdom."[7]

Paul points to actual demonstrations of man's foolishness (vv. 22, 23). One example is the Jews. They sought God in tradition, in the letter of the Law. They demanded evidence and visible positive affirmation and were interested in the practical. Yet they framed God in and offered Jesus only one pattern to fit. Then they stumbled over the fact of a crucified Messiah because it was not a "good sign." This ruined their expectations. The other example is the Greeks. These were absorbed in speculative philosophy, as Acts 17:21 points out. They were intellectual beings and proud of their reasoning. This left no place for God because their reasoning did not allow true faith; consequently, they considered the Cross ridiculous.

Despite this, the preaching of the cross of Christ has great

23

effect. It changes people, calls them to faith, and unites and crosses all man-made boundaries, for it is the direct revelation and plan of God. Man is depicted in all of his wisdom and brilliance. He is shown in the strength of his work. But man, with his highest achievements, cannot touch God. But the gospel reveals God and demonstrates His power to all generations.

C. The Choice of Weak Vessels (1:26-31)

Because the Cross was considered foolish by many, God's call was really heard by the weak and foolish, those who needed Him. Within the context, Paul reminds the Corinthians of their own calling and experience. Paul explains "wise men after the flesh" (v. 26) with what immediately follows. Not many "mighty" men or men of influence, men of rank and government, are chosen. Not many "noble" men, or men of high birth (or, in particular here, men of Roman citizenship by heredity) are called. Notice that Paul says some of these men are chosen, but not many. It may be their position in life has made the simple faith for salvation difficult. In a sense Paul is asking, "If the gospel had been a grand philosophy, would he have addressed it to fools and weaklings?"[8] This serves to hit at the Corinthians' pride and remind them of the world's estimate of them. They were trying to have the world's approval, when they should have been seeking only God's good pleasure.

But God does nothing because of capriciousness or because He can get nothing better. He had a purpose in His calling. God chose the weak and lowly. The world may laugh, but it is God himself who has done the choosing. It must be added that not only does the world consider these weak and foolish; they really are! What a blow to pride! Yet Paul goes further (v. 28). He calls these "base" or low-born and the opposite of noble. He calls them "despised," which Knox translates as "contemptible."[9]

God chose these apparently insignificant ones to shame and confuse the strong; to reduce to insignificance the great of the world. In so doing, He expressed His love, in that He would willingly choose and lift the lowly and ugly. God has done this so "no flesh," including all of mankind, could boast before Him. God has refuted the so-called wisdom of this world, and the

24

Church is nothing without the Lord; thus, no one can say, "My own right arm is my salvation and strength."

Paul then turns to the opposite side of the argument and reveals that we are nevertheless blessed and rich because of the work of Jesus Christ. The debased are now exalted by the apostle. But this time the exaltation is real and comes on the right foundation. We are blessed because we are "in Christ." It is to be noted in passing that Paul presents the work of Christ here as also made the work of the Father (v. 30). Christ is made to all believers "wisdom," which stands alone and may be explained by the last three words. There is a reference to the content of life from God. He turned the world's wisdom to foolishness for our salvation. Christ is our "righteousness,"[10] our "sanctification,"[11] and our "redemption."[12] Our life in God is grounded in Jesus Christ. Yet underlying this is the theme developed from the beginning, that being "in Christ" will produce union and fellowship with others who are also "in Christ."

When a man discovers the merits and riches of Christ, he will glorify Him[13] for this great revelation of wisdom and power. No other name could be placed alongside the name of Jesus (see v. 12), for Paul refers to Jeremiah 9:23, 24 where the reference is to Jehovah, and transfers this idea to Christ; placing Him above all other names (except God the Father) and personalities. Jesus Christ is Lord.

D. The Power of the Gospel (2:1-5)

"And I" (v. 1) begins to express the truth of chapter 1. When Paul came to them, probably from Athens, he came not as the usual itinerant professor of wisdom, with which the Corinthians were so familiar. Rather, his preaching was determined by the will of God and perpetuated by the power of God. To enlarge upon the idea, Paul reminds his readers of how he did *not* preach. Despite the comments of some modern expositors, it is entirely possible that Paul did have oratorical ability. But if he did, he made it a point not to use it at Corinth. Nor did he try to make the message sound humanly brilliant. He spoke in presentation and content rather plainly.[14] He came in "weakness,"[15] in fear,[16] and in trembling.[17] The haughty are now informed that Paul worked

25

without a sense of self-sufficiency. Yet the results were excellent. Paul preached with power and the Word was confirmed by God. The premise on which he stood was true; the promises he declared were true; the power with which he spoke was true. The only logical result was the persuasion of men concerning Christ and the enlargement of His kingdom.

Paul's writing in this vein is clearly applied in verse 5. If these believers stood on what someone said through his wisdom only, in time, the foundation would crumble. This world's wisdom will fail, and so will those who stand upon it. But if these believers rested in God they would not fall or fail. Faith in God's wisdom as displayed in Christ will not only produce maturity but also miracles.

E. Spiritual vs. Natural Wisdom (2:6-16)

Paul continues to demolish step by step the foundation of natural wisdom on which the Corinthians were attempting to build. In thus comparing spiritual wisdom with natural wisdom, Paul notes that among "perfect" or "full-grown" believers the gospel is recognized as wisdom (v. 6). These mature thinkers have freed themselves from the world and its values and so can acknowledge and pursue truth. God's wisdom is not dependent on the world, for it is permanent, and the world is on its way to a foolish, nonsensical end. True wisdom is not governed by leaders who set the patterns of this world in general. Yet while noting that this simple gospel is free from human additives, we must also recognize that in another sense it is the most brilliant "philosophy" to ever appear.

Because it does not come from men it appears as a mystery, a secret which man by himself could never unfold. But when Paul uses it in his epistles he uses it in the sense of something long hidden, but now revealed. Indeed, when Christ came the mystery of the gospel was unfolded by God himself. Thus, Paul tells the Corinthians that while they have been flirting with the idea of abandoning this simple wisdom, in reality they are possessors of great benefits and the only real wisdom in all the world—the wisdom and power of God in Christ. And to add the frosting to the cake, Paul declares that in the dim realms of eternity, before creation itself, God ordained this wisdom to be for our good and

26

glory, that we might know, enjoy, and partake of the glory that is Christ's.

The "princes of this world"[18] did not know God's plans or revelation. They did not really understand the need and importance of salvation. If they had understood God's wise plan, they would have never crucified Christ, who was the wisdom of God incarnate. "Known" (v. 8) carries the idea of acknowledgment and so involves man's will. The implication is that God in His foreknowledge knew man would crucify Christ and worked it to man's hope or shame depending on personal choice. In any case, Christ, the "Lord of Glory," One of great position and title, would not have been crucified by wise men. In passing, our position (see v. 7) is also noted by this term *Lord of Glory,* a position by association.

That the plan of God would be a mystery was foretold by Scripture. Paul quotes from Isaiah 64:4 and 65:17 (v. 9). He refers to wonders beyond the senses, perception, or imagination of men.[19] It took a specific revelation by the Holy Spirit for us to understand the wisdom of God. This verse does not refer to future glories to be still unfolded, but to wonders already shown to us (see v. 10). Christ comes from God and so does the recognition of Him. Living in spiritual darkness, the Holy Spirit must show us that Christ is the wisdom of God.

This the Holy Spirit can do because He "searches" the things of God. This is basic. The word *searches* does not suggest incompleteness, but rather the opposite—fullness of knowledge, action, and penetration. He searches the deep things of God. Salvation belongs here, but much more than just initial salvation is seen. Included is wisdom, knowledge, and judgment—the work of the Holy Spirit and God himself.

Paul magnifies his discussion with an illustration (v. 11). From a human viewpoint, only the spirit of a man knows and understands the inner thoughts of a man. In other words, there are secrets kept from others. The comparison is made with the Spirit of God. But a point of clarification must be offered. "Spirit of man" refers to ego or self-consciousness. The "Spirit of God" could not be God's self-consciousness because this would take away the Spirit's personality and individuality. But the point of comparison is that He can know that which no one except God could know. Only the Holy Spirit can recognize, understand, and reveal the heart and mind of God.

Now man may know the "things . . . of God" (v. 12) because, and only because, he has received the Spirit of God. We have not received the "spirit of the world," which here refers not to Satan but to something human, an attitude, a temper. Instead, in a reference that may allude to Pentecost and the historic coming of the Holy Spirit,[20] we have received the Holy Spirit. He was sent that we might understand, discern, and possess the gifts of God. Grace can only be understood through the eyes of the Spirit. Again notice the emphasis on God's free decision to allow us to know these deeper things of God. To know true wisdom and the gifts of God, the presence of the Holy Spirit is essential and mandatory.

Closely connected with knowledge (v. 12) is speaking (v. 13). There will come from the spiritual man spiritual things. Verse 13 points to what Christians endowed with the Spirit are always doing, for the verbs are in the present tense. These "spiritual" words have a definite color and lead in a definite direction. Thus, Christians do speak what the world does not often understand. There is a comparison of "spiritual things[21] with spiritual."[22]

Again, lest there be arguments in the minds of his readers, Paul compares the natural man and the spiritual man (v. 14). The distinction made is both absolute and general. It would seem that a total ignorance and rejection of "all" spiritual things is here suggested. Man calls the gospel nonsense because he has not received the Spirit to enlighten him, and he cannot by reason find out these things; they must be revealed. A deaf man cannot accurately "judge" music; a blind man cannot accurately "judge" the landscape; a natural man cannot receive or discern or "judge" spiritual things.

But the spiritual man is able to "judge" or compare, combine, and examine all things (v. 15) because his source of wisdom is completely accurate. The basis for this is found in verse 10. This is not to say, however, that the Christian believer would express knowledge on every single area of knowledge. We must confine ourselves at this point to the context. Yet he is permitted to "judge." Since the believer is part of the world, however, his judgment would involve secular as well as sacred. In judging the world's direction, philosophy, and attitude, some men are led to despair and even suicide. But as the Christian compares, examines, and in this specific sense "judges" but does not condemn, he is led to see the hope and victory for the man in Christ Jesus. At the same time, it is impossible for the natural man to make a similar judgment on the Christian, for he has no accurate source of knowledge.

With verse 16 Paul lists a proof for verse 15. By his question (to which he expects a particular answer), he tells us no man has ever given the Lord instruction, counsel, or advice, and no natural man is able to ascend to God or find out anything about Him outside of divine revelation. (The quotation is from Isaiah 40:13.) Rather, a gift from God by His Spirit must come. That gift is the mind of Christ, to know and understand. Thus, a mystical union is presented, a marvelous work of grace is shown, and a deeper dimension of the Spirit's control and work is understood. God has come to be in us.

F. The Need for Maturity in Christian Labor (3:1-9)

But, alas, these brethren at Corinth, with whom Paul had a personal and loving relationship were not mature, spiritual men (v. 1). Up to this point in his discussion on wisdom Paul has been more general. Now he becomes very specific and pointed. When Paul had come to Corinth God had blessed, and these men had become spiritual "babes." They were young and weak. There is nothing wrong with that. Every Christian begins without experience, with little understanding; the need is for growth. But as we will shortly see, this entire section suggests the incapacity of the unspiritual for spiritual things, and these had become "carnal" Christians. They had no capacity for spiritual things because they had not grown and thus were "unspiritual."

In point of fact, Paul began his ministry by feeding them milk. Paul is not saying he fed them on anything but the principles of Christ, but remember there is a realm in God that young Christians do not know and are not yet ready for. This soft diet had been necessary because their spiritual bodies were not old enough or strong enough for a regular diet. And at this point (v. 2) Paul levels the terrible charge. They had been babes; that was all right.

29

But they had *remained* babes; they had not grown one bit. They remained on the same plateau as when they had first begun and so proved themselves "carnal Christians." This was a real rebuke to the pride and sense of accomplishment of the Corinthians.

Verse 3 explains what is meant by verses 1 and 2. The word *carnal* in verse 1 is different from "carnal" in verse 3.[23] The first word means "fleshy" or fleshly and one *cannot* help it. The second means "fleshly" and one *will not* help it. They should have been bearing the fruit of the Spirit; instead they were bearing the fruit of the flesh. This was particularly true as it applied to divisions in the church. Divisions were not only bad; they also proved the immaturity of the church members. The feelings of jealousy and the words and actions of strife[24] proved their inclination toward natural, worldly living.

With strong words Paul attacks this specific arm of the problem. He attacks those in particular who follow him and Apollos. He may have done this to prove his own unworthiness; and he may have used Apollos because he was a close friend at Ephesus with him. Or, these could have been the two strongest parties or the most quarrelsome. The question of verse 4 is obviously intended to gain a positive answer.

The mature laborer for Christ does not involve himself in party dissension. The men whom God uses for work in His kingdom are really servants called to bring men to belief in Christ.[25] God had given each minister a particular work, ability, and ministry which He used with the Word to bring the Corinthians to salvation. The emphasis is on God. As John wrote in his Gospel concerning John the Baptist: "There was a man sent from God, whose name was John" (1:6).

Paul introduces the illustration (v. 6) of a farmer or gardener. Paul had initiated the work; Apollos had strengthened and nurtured it. But these men had cooperated together under the direction of God, for it was God alone who gave the increase or harvest. The first two verbs of this verse are aorist and point to work already done. But God's activity is in the imperfect tense and indicates work continuing after a specific beginning.

Such divisions in the church cannot be allowed because the leaders and laborers are mere instruments. God accomplishes (v. 7) through them what He will. The Christian worker must main-

tain the humility, submission, and unity that come from understanding that all men work in the place God calls them to and all
are important under God.

Every minister and laborer then is on an equal plane. The job
does not exalt one more than another. All share a common goal.
Therefore, the reward given to these subordinates will be dependent on their personal labor. The emphasis seems to be on the
labor not the success; on the faithfulness of the servant involved.
"We are laborers together with God."[26] The emphasis is on God;
He is mentioned emphatically three times in verse 9. We are in
keeping with the figures already suggested, God's husbandry[27]
and God's building;[28] God's possession then is in close view. If
these Corinthians came to see God's proper place here then they
would also come to see His ministers' proper place. To summarize, three results would be accomplished: these readers (and
we also) would come to a true view of human teachers, and would
listen to them but not idolize them; we would not mistreat God's
workers because they belong to God; and we would not mistreat
ourselves because we belong to God.

G. The Test of a Builder's Work (3:10-15)

So then men as colaborers with God build for Him. Paul
indeed had done this. As a master builder, architect, and superin-
tendent, he had skillfully laid a foundation (vv. 10, 11). Luke 6:49
indicates that the unskillful lay no foundation. But Paul guards
against usurping divine glory for he indicates that his wise building was due to the grace of God and not his own abilities. "It is no
crime in a Christian, but much to his commendation, to take
notice of the good that is in him, to the praise of divine grace."[29]

As we continue, Paul will introduce three classes of builders:
(1) those who are truly wise; (2) those who are unwise and introduce wrong material but do not leave the foundation; and (3)
those who are fools and try to destroy God's temple. Paul will
acknowledge other builders besides himself, but he will acknowledge no foundation other than Jesus Christ. Everything must be
built on the person and doctrine of Christ. In an absolute sense,
there can be no other foundation.

In building, men will use different materials. Paul lists at least

31

two categories of materials—good materials and bad materials. But he also sets the stage for his next figure, fire, by listing three incombustible and three combustible types of material (v. 12). These materials have been said to refer to one of three areas: (1) different sorts of persons in the Church; (2) moral fruits; and (3) doctrines of the different teachers. It seems difficult and impractical to finely distinguish between the three possibilities, since they have a joint effect on each other. There is, however, some emphasis on speculative, curious doctrine versus solid doctrine. One thing is certain, the emphasis is on what is done, not how it is done.

Whatever is built will be tested (v. 13). This is clear teaching of a definite judgment of Christian works. "Day" and "fire" both refer to the final judgment and there is no basis here for the doctrine of purgatory. This is a purging fire. The intent of the fire is to prove the value and good of the item tested. Sadly, that will be untrue in some cases.

On the basis of the test, the builder will receive his reward (vv. 14, 15). If good has come out of the fire of judgment then he shall receive his honest and just wages. But what is built must be of the strongest materials to withstand the fire.[30] Note that the reward is conditional. If a man builds with the wrong materials, then he shall lose his reward but still merit eternal life. Apparently this individual built with the wrong materials on the right foundation. It must be said, however, that there appears to be a very fine line between the foolish builder of verse 15 and the destroyer of verse 17.

H. The Care of God's Temple (3:16, 17)

The reason for the mason's care was that this building was God's temple, the habitation of God's Spirit. This carries a collective meaning (v. 16). (The thought regarding the individual is better indicated in 1 Corinthians 6:19, 20.) "Know ye not" suggests something the Corinthians should have remembered but had forgotten. The temple[31] was the noblest of buildings, for it was consecrated to the highest purposes—the pursuit and worship of Almighty God.

The man who would destroy (v. 17) this building, then, would reap the most terrible of punishments. Actions are joined together here. The reason this man would be destroyed is that he attempted to destroy the temple of God. No man may touch the Church in this way without paying for it. God will not allow evil to taint His possession for He is holy and His own must be holy. In spite of her failures, the Church is blessed with great glory.

I. God's Wisdom and Man's Pride (3:18-23)

If so much emphasis must be placed on God, then man must take his proper place. To believe oneself to be wise is really dangerous self-deception. The word *seemeth* (v. 18) is better translated "thinketh." This is an obvious reference to those who thought themselves wise, attaching themselves to a certain teacher. The source of such self-deceit is pride. The antidote to such pride is humility which fosters a dependence on a higher source. A man cannot be wise in both the world and the Church. The world thinks all Christian wisdom is foolish and vice versa. At the heart of wisdom is the Cross. Either a man will despise it or cling to it. If he holds to it, he will gain much. If he despises it, he will become a tragic figure.

As God looks at man's wisdom from the viewpoint of its inability to discover and attain salvation, He considers it utter nonsense. The wisdom of the world is thought to be foolish by God. More than that, it is *proven* to be foolish by God; God intervenes and brings it to nothing. How is this proven? Look at Scripture.

Paul quotes first from Job 5:13 (v. 19). It is not an exact quotation but more of a summary. The words were spoken by Eliphaz. They were given a wrong application by the speaker, but the apostle does not speak about the application. He uses the words themselves, which concerning God are true. God catches the crafty and exposes them. They are brought face to face with the fact that His wisdom outranks theirs totally. Then Paul quotes from Psalm 94:11 (v. 20). He does substitute "the wise" for "man" and "vain" for "vanity" here, possibly quoting from some manuscript we do not know about. Nonetheless, the thought is clear. "The Lord knoweth" carries with it the idea of total knowledge. No thought, even the most secret, is hidden from God. This is part of the reason why the Lord can intervene in the plans of men.

33

He knows their thoughts from the very beginning. Their worldly ideas are vain or, if you please, futile, hollow, and useless.

We are, therefore, led to a natural conclusion. Let no man glory in or boast of other men or himself (v. 21). The creation must not be elevated above the Creator. After all, with the Christian such action is not necessary. He has already been blessed in every way in Christ. There is no limit to the possession of the Christian in Christ. In reality, Paul is not so much arguing against the lifting up of men as he is presenting the idea that these Corinthians were limiting themselves. Why should they listen to only one teacher, when all the teachers in their different aspects and different approaches were given to benefit the Church? In listening to only one man, the Corinthians were limiting their potential and limiting the resources of God to them personally. But Paul does not stop there. He enlarges the circle to include certain riches that would possess special value and interest to the church to which he is writing (vv. 22, 23). These items fall into natural groups.

The first group consists of Christian ministers and teachers. There was Paul with his unique presentation of the gospel; his logical, anointed, and highly singular ministry. There was Apollos with his brilliant rhetoric, lofty phraseology, and outstanding oratory. There was Cephas or Peter with his fond memories of personal acquaintance with Christ on earth. Why should the Corinthians despise two and listen to only one when all three were given by God?

The second group consists of the world, life, and death. "World" refers to the ordered universe, to the physical universe, and to the universe in which we live. "Life" is really the spiritual life in Christ Jesus. Life in Christ is the only real life and the Christian possesses this. Philippians 1:21 offers meaning to this: "To me to live is Christ, and to die is gain." "Death," an apparent obstacle to man and a word filled with pain, sorrow, and the unknown, is really our servant because Christ conquered death. It is the messenger by which our spirit is carried to the heavenly world.

The last group is things present and things to come. Not all things in the present seem to be to our benefit, but in reality they are. They all accomplish the purposes of God. "Things to come" includes a vast array of unknown blessings, as well as eternal life.

The idea conveyed is one of complete and ultimate triumph. Paul sums it all up with a repetition of the words, "all are yours."

At the very end of this soaring idea Paul places the foundation. We are laid at the feet of Christ (v. 23). It is an entirely different idea for us to be in Christ and to be richly blessed, than it is to be possessors of certain riches. We are the stewards of certain riches and we are possessions of Christ. So we return again to the idea of ownership and Christ's mastery over us. "You" or "ye" wipes out all thought of remote individuality or division. Paul must convey here the idea of our responsibility as Christians and members of Christ's church and of our submission to the total authority of Christ in God. Our subordination to Christ is given a supreme example in Christ's subordination to God. In other places Paul asserts the deity of Christ and the equality of each Member of the Trinity. He is not here taking away anything from that idea. Rather, he is referring to the office of Christ. In that sense, Christ is subject to God, because it was God's call and initiative that sent Christ on His mission.[32] Thus, Paul reaches the mountaintop of his argument, but much of importance must follow in the discussion. Everything that comes into our lives we can master, because we are servants of Christ, who in work is the servant of the Father, who is Lord over all.

J. The Stewardship of the Gospel (4:1-5)

To us, then, who are both servants and masters in Christ, comes the acknowledgment of stewardship. This is the practical outgrowth of unity, wisdom, and service. Paul declares himself to be a "minister of Christ."[33] He does it for a purpose. While Paul may have been too highly valued by some, which created a party spirit, nevertheless, he establishes that he is a minister and should not be considered too lightly. There is a happy medium in the discussion. Ministers are not lords, but they are stewards of the gospel of Christ, once a divine mystery. And this deserves honor and respect. The Church comprises the house; God is the Head of the house; the members of the house make up the household; and the apostles were the stewards[34] of the house.

It is required in the very nature of such a man and steward that he be faithful to his work. As he has been doing, Paul reproves the

35

pride and disunity of the Corinthians by indicating that ultimately the test of a steward is not his "ability" but his faithfulness.
A steward is expected to act in the interest of his master, not in his
own interest. And such is the requirement of all stewards, not just
some, because this faithfulness will come to light at some time. A
steward is not always closely supervised. But he is expected to
carry on his duties carefully nonetheless.

Lest the Corinthians get the idea from 3:22 that they could
judge these stewards, Paul adds that neither they nor any other
steward could judge another man's fidelity (v. 3). In fact, not even
Paul's own conscience was the final judge. Paul is not rejecting the
importance of other men's ideas and opinions, nor is he rejecting
the place of conscience. He is simply comparing inferior with
superior. Other men are often fickle and prejudiced in their
examination, and a man may find it difficult to be objective and
honest with himself. Heart searching is advised by Scripture, but
there is such a thing as too much self-examination. As far as Paul
knows he has done his best and therefore knows no reason for
condemnation (v. 4). But he freely admits his knowledge is limited.

No, He that judgeth is the Master, the Lord himself. Paul is
justified on the basis of Christ's righteousness. As Titus 3:5-8
indicates, this is the basis of his whole stand before God. Good
conscience is fine, but it cannot be relied on apart from the verdict
of Christ. The appraisement at the end will come from Him who
justified at the beginning. Therefore, for the present, Paul leaves
to Christ the testing of his daily course; which Christ is doing in
preparation for the final judgment. Some feel that even in verse 4
Paul is speaking of future judgment, but this would ruin his
grammar and upset the rock of his present stand before God and
men.

When, therefore, we come to the natural conclusion (v. 5), we
must understand Paul is not forbidding "proving" and examin-
ing, but he is objecting to the proud judgment of teachers and the
usurping of Christ's position. Only the Lord can judge correctly.
He can do so because the hidden things of darkness shall be
brought to light. This entails the unknown, secret things now
covered. These shall be brought to exposure by the light of
Christ's presence. The Lord shall make manifest the counsels and

purposes of the heart. This speaks of the real, central inner nature of a man. "Counsels" is neuter, indicating good or evil. Each shall then receive his due praise from God. Only God can judge honestly; thus, only God can praise honestly. Paul speaks here of the positive side. Enough has been said of the negative in 3:15-17. Also involved in the thinking of Paul would be the work of fellow ministers such as Apollos and Peter for whom he has high regard. He throws no blame on them.

K. The Example of the Apostles (4:6-13)

Paul uses a literary figure to refer what he has just said to himself and Apollos that they might serve as illustrations of his point. The example is intended to help the Corinthians quell their pride and teach them not to lift men out of place. "That which is written" (v. 6) has had many interpretations. Some have said this refers to what Paul has already written. But the phrase seems more proverbial. It is difficult to find any particular Scripture passage that Paul is drawing from. Consequently, it probably has reference to Scripture in general or perhaps to the Old Testament.[35] Paul makes this general reference to Scripture so that through this example the Corinthians will learn the subordination of man. The Bible exalts God. The Corinthians were exalting man. Paul will come at this issue from many sides, taking us ever deeper until we have come to the heart of the matter and covered all of the ramifications. In this spirit of pride the Corinthians had made judgments on their teachers, and in adhering to one had denounced all the others.

With three rhetorical questions Paul attacks the problem (v. 7). The first question hits the fact that some of the Corinthians considered themselves superior in some way. Paul asserts that this partisan conceit is presumptuous. The question demands an answer that cuts away at pride. The second question really answers the first. The Corinthians had received all they had from God. They had no right to boast and think they had obtained their position by their own hand. The third question goes a step further. They could not boast as if they had not been given what they had; in so doing, they were glorifying themselves and reveling in conceit.

The dark characterization continues (v. 8). "Full" and "rich" denote the satisfaction and attainment the Corinthians felt. Having come to an ultimate plateau, they did not need the apostles or recognize them as necessary. All this accomplishment had been done by their own hands. Luther comments: "Paul mocks them, for he means the opposite of what he says."[36] The truth is, they had not attained. Paul wishes they had, because he knows in God's plan the apostles would share their inheritance. But the apostles are doing anything but reigning and the Corinthians are not either.

Paul establishes the position of the apostles and himself (v. 9) quickly and it is far from what the Corinthians imagined it to be. It seems as though the apostles are last in line and like men "appointed to death." In Paul's time criminals condemned to death were exhibited to amuse the crowds in the amphitheater. Then they were brought to the arena to fight wild beasts; they did not leave the arena alive. These men were exhibited to the crowds; the apostles were exhibited to the world. This world consists of angels (which in comparison to men are not specifically noted as good or bad) and men (which might include good and bad).

Then Paul specifically compares the apostles and the Corinthians (v. 10). The combination of "we" and "ye" is important. The opinion of the world is that the apostles are fanatical and foolish. Meanwhile, the Corinthians are supposed to be wise. In Christ the Corinthians really are wise, but they were building on the wisdom of the world, which Paul has already refuted. "For Christ" and "in Christ" carry a shade of distinction and meaning which shows the depth of the apostles' work. The world may have given some honor to this church because it desired it and had gone after it, but the apostles preached only Christ and so received dishonor from the world.

The list of difficulties continues (vv. 11-13). The apostles were enduring trials for the gospel even to the moment of writing. Paul may be reminded of what he is undergoing at Ephesus. They had little food, little liquid, little clothing; they were beaten with fists and whips; and they were vagabonds. To Paul's tender and sensitive nature this hurt. As far as this world was concerned, they had little or nothing, and they supported themselves by work that was exhausting. Again, this was for Christ and His church. To the

38

Greeks, manual labor was low and insulting and so were those who did it.

But through all this, the apostles retained their love and joy. When cursed, they blessed by giving the gospel generally and specifically; when wrongly treated, they endured patiently and lovingly; when slandered and lied about, they encouraged, exhorted, and quietly pleaded their case. And the present participles indicate continuation.

But the picture is not quite finished. They are regarded as "filth"[37] and "offscouring."[38] Beyond this Paul does not or cannot go. Again the present and continuous is indicated by "unto this day" (even until now). All of this is in opposition to the self-assertive spirit of the world and the self-sufficient, self-possessed spirit of the Corinthians. Paul and others had sacrificed everything for Jesus, that the plan of salvation would be known to all men.

L. The Admonitions of a "Spiritual Father" (4:14-21)

In what Paul has just written, it has not been his aim to shame or embarrass. Rather, he wishes to bring his readers to reason, to give them counsel, to make them understand their true position in Christ and the world and how foolish their pride and bigotry are. That is a painful lesson. Paul shows his deep feelings for them by calling them his "beloved sons" (v. 14). Their wrong actions and attitudes had touched Paul deeply.

Paul had been strongly aroused by the Corinthians' behavior, yet the rebuke of verse 14 is mild. Verse 15 helps explain why. The readers had had many "instructors" or "tutors" (ASV).[39] "Ten thousand" may well be an exaggeration, but it emphasizes Paul's point. Paul lays claim to the right to especially admonish and to be especially heeded because, unlike these other instructors, he was their spiritual father. How does he claim this? He was the one who first brought the gospel to Corinth. It was through him (by Christ) that the church there was founded and by his preaching many of the converts there first met Christ. Spiritual fatherhood carries with it a solemn obligation and Paul is fulfilling that by admonishing the Corinthians to godly living and by correcting them.

39

Paul continues the father-child figure (vv. 16, 17) by urging that as a child follows a father so they should follow him. It is a mark of Paul's deeply spiritual life that he could ask the Corinthians to imitate his example. We must set limitations, though, and say that Paul meant his example in Christ Jesus. This will not stir up divisions again. It is one thing to say, "I am of Paul," and quite another to follow in Paul's steps as he points to the Master.

Because he had so much concern for the welfare of the Corinthians, Paul had sent Timothy to admonish and encourage them in the Lord. Timothy was on his way, traveling by land before Paul wrote 1 Corinthians, but the letter, traveling by sea, would arrive first. It is difficult to believe Timothy carried this letter.

We have a small profile on Timothy here. He was like a son, greatly loved by Paul. It may be Paul had a part in Timothy's salvation. Certainly he influenced his spiritual maturation. And Timothy was a faithful Christian, true to his calling.

Timothy's purpose was to remind the Corinthians of Paul's actions and teachings in Christ. It is difficult to say exactly how this was to happen, but perhaps it would be by Timothy's teaching and life. In doing this, Paul was being very fair, for his life and doctrine remained constant—they began in Christ and ended there. He did not teach a different message according to the crowd, but everywhere proclaimed the same thing.

Because Timothy had been sent and Paul had not come, some had become proud and said Paul was afraid to face them (vv. 18-21). It may be they hoped he would not come, so they had convinced themselves that he would not. Paul sets the record straight. He would come, provided the Lord so directed; which is all any servant can say. In coming, he would not be interested in their speeches but in their effectiveness, their power. Again we are reminded that the gospel is not mere theory, but practice; with power to make that practice effective.[40] We are also reminded of the comparisons Paul has already made between words (1:17) and power (1:24), and between excellency of speech (2:1) and power (2:4).

Verse 20 supplies the base for verse 19. The Corinthians must show God's power in their lives because the kingdom of God is not in word, but power and deed. Thus, Paul not only reveals the objective nature of the kingdom of God, but he also condemns pride. There is a contrast between this verse and the claims of Paul's readers in 4:8. It is also interesting to note that in 2 Corinthians 13:1-10, Paul applies this same test to himself.

Thus, the decision is left to the Corinthians. Paul has been stirred by what he has already written and by what he is about to write. But how he will come to them will be determined by their future actions. He can come with sharpness and discipline, albeit in love, or he can come in love and gentleness, with a special manifestation of his care and regard for them.

With these words we come to the end of this major section. At the heart of division is pride. The antidote is the love of Christ working with and in us, with the discipline that accompanies it. Our lives are wrapped up in God; our salvation is from God; our labor must be for God.

III

Indifference
in
Social Morality
(5:1 to 6:20)

A. Disciplining an Offender (5:1-8)

The case of incest is very serious, but Paul could not treat it until he had spoken to the problem of division. Church discipline could not be handled by a disunited church.

Without preamble, Paul steps into the next problem: indifference toward immorality. Incest was an undoubted, talked-about fact (v. 1). "Fornication" normally denotes participation with a harlot, but here Paul uses it in the form of general sexual misconduct. This particular conduct is incest. While this was not entirely unknown among the Gentiles, Paul indicates that it was not common and definitely not condoned. It was not even named or mentioned among them; being too shameful. Both Greek and Roman law stamped this with infamy and Jewish law stated harsh penalties for this act.[41]

The sin was between a man and his "father's wife." It has been suggested this refers to a stepmother, that the offender had seduced his stepmother, or that she was divorced, or the father had died, leaving her a widow.[42] Such specifics are not stated. We only know this disgraceful union had been established and, as "should have" tells us, it was a continued relationship.

Alas, the reaction of the church had been sadly amiss. The Corinthians' pride had reached such a point that they considered themselves above the standard of God. Perhaps they considered themselves properly broad-minded. They were not sorrowful over their own indifference and reproach. Pride had blinded them again to their true position and to what should have been their action. Paul indicates that they should expel the sinner. He does not indicate how; apparently the church knew. The honor of God and the holiness of the church were at stake.

Paul's judgment (vv. 3-5) is clear and a sharp contrast to that of the Corinthians. He thought of himself as present "in spirit." Having characterized the man by his deed, Paul disciplines with authority. The verb is in the perfect, which adds an air of finality.[43] Certainly Paul's knowledge and judgment of this matter were aided by the Holy Spirit.

While the church should have done something long ago, it had not. Paul's judgment must prompt the church to expel the sinner. Yet by this Paul has in mind the welfare of the sinner as well as the purity of the church, as will be seen shortly. Paul has recorded a judgment; the main action must now come from the church.

"In the name of our Lord Jesus,"[44] which is probably best connected with "to deliver . . . one" (v. 5), is the opening for a solemn judicial sentence and tells us under what authority all proper church gatherings and administrations must operate.

"When ye are gathered together" probably is associated with "with the power of our Lord Jesus," and indicates that this is not to be a minority meeting, but the gathering of the whole church to perform a solemn act. Paul would be there "in spirit" heading the proceedings. If the Corinthians had called his spirit and teachings to remembrance and followed them, this discussion would have been unnecessary. "With" (v. 4) suggests not only Christ's power and presence will be there, but also His cooperation. It must also be noted that Paul does not try to make his presence and Christ's presence co-equal. The proceedings must be in Christ's authority and for His glory. His presence is necessary with Paul's spirit and the congregation, to make the sentence valid.

The purpose of this sentence is discussed in verse 5. "Delivering to Satan" has two major views. Many suggest it means excommunication; thrusting him out into the world of darkness where Satan holds sway.[45] Others argue against this because of the phrase "for the destruction of the flesh," and suggest this means some physical affliction and spiritual visitation of the guilty. In support of this are the following: "Flesh" (v. 5) refers to the bodily nature. Physical maladies and even death are ascribed to Satan in the New Testament (Luke 13:16; John 8:44; 2 Corinthians 12:7; Hebrews 2:14), and sickness is often the result of being withdrawn from the secure realm of fellowship with God. Affliction is made an instrument of spiritual benefit (9:27; 11:30-32; 2 Corin-

44

thians 4:16-18; 12:7; 1 Peter 4). The apostles did on occasion pronounce penal sentences in the physical realm (Acts 5:1-10; 13:1-12). And sending a man back to the world would appear to strengthen rather than destroy fleshly passions.

Therefore, many support physical affliction instead of "excommunication."[46] However, one difficulty with this view is that in certain cases there seems to be an attempt to separate body and spirit, in opposition to 1 Corinthians 15. It has also been suggested that Paul may have in mind the idea of letting the flesh go as far as it can in Satan's realm, and then the sinner will remember God's goodness and return. This would be most precarious, and "flesh" would then have to refer to "man's lower nature and lusts."

But we do know the intent of the sentence: to bring the offender back to Christ that on the "day of the Lord," when every man's position shall be finalized, he will stand with the company of the redeemed. One note should be added: in this account Satan is pictured as subject to God, and God will gain final glory in every situation.

Having given this situation attention, Paul returns to the root of the problem, pride, and plainly states that the resultant boasting of the Corinthians is wrong (v. 6). Strictly speaking, the word *glorying* suggests content not action. What Paul is really upset about here is what they were bragging about. He uses the illustration of yeast in bread to make his point. It takes only a little yeast to cause bread to rise. The application is that both the church as a whole and the individual, in allowing evil, would in time corrupt the whole Christian community, collectively and individually. Rot spreads quickly. Once again, starting with a specific situation, Paul has come to the Corinthian attitude in general.

The command is, therefore, to clean out the evil (probably meaning the pride and boasting; v. 7). With that Paul reminds them of another figure. Certain ceremonies preceded the eating of the Passover meal. For 7 days Israel ate unleavened bread, having removed the leaven from their homes on the first day. This was to remind them of the great Exodus and the liberation from the sins of Egypt. What the Israelites used on their journey was quite different from that used in Egypt. The application of the illustration is this: Too much of the heathen life-style remained with the Corinthians. They should be new, fresh, and free in Christ. The emphasis is that the Corinthians ought to remove the leaven.

The figure is expanded. Israel ate the unleavened bread after the Passover. Christ as the paschal lamb enables His people to be ever unleavened. Believers are free from sins objectively and, subjectively, called to remove all remaining sins. Christ had made them free from corruption and the Corinthians had no business allowing old "yeast" to reenter the "new lump."

Paul therefore exhorts them to keep the feast (v. 8), not literally, but symbolically; not with the leaven of malice and wickedness, but with the unleavened bread of sincerity and truth. "Let us keep" is present continuous and indicates a continued operation. "Malice" refers to the evil habit of mind and "wickedness" to the outcome of that mind. Contrasted with it is purity of mind and motive ("sincerity") and purity of action ("truth"). Purity must be retained in the church. Christ is our example in this. If He is also our life, the gospel will have its effect in us and out of us.

B. Separating From Evil "Brothers" (5:9-13)

This subject had apparently come up before (v. 9). We do not have this epistle, but it seems "fornication" (which is again a general term) was a problem the church at Corinth had repeated difficulty with. The order had been to forbid social intimacy with those who indulged in such practices.

But now Paul discovers a problem had arisen with this in an opposite direction (v. 10). A misunderstanding had developed over the force and purpose of Paul's command, and now these believers claimed that what was meant was separation in a way that was impossible. But Paul does not mean avoiding contact with sinners in a general way. That would require leaving the world; otherwise, such absence of contact was impossible. Yet, Paul contends that in many circumstances his readers should not participate in the activities of those who do not obey the Lord. He notes some of those who do not work to glorify God. Along with "fornicators," which we have discussed, Paul lists the "covetous," who are possessed by a greedy desire to have more; "extortioners" (closely linked with the "covetous" by a single article), who take what is not theirs (robbers in any form); and "idolaters," who worship the wrong things. It should be noted that the relationship of the church to these worldly men is different from that of a Christian brother to them; thus, Paul can write this.

Paul makes clear then his meaning of "separation" (vv. 11-13). The Corinthians could control who they made deep friendships with and whether or not evil pervaded their fellowship. "I wrote" allows a stronger possibility for meaning the present letter, but this is unnecessary. The kingdom of God is not of this world and cannot be carried out by worldly associations. It is preserved by the power of God. If one who professes himself a Christian is really involved in evil living he cannot be an intimate friend. And to the list in verse 10 Paul adds the "railer," who abuses others, and the "drunkard," which speaks for itself.

"Not to eat" (v. 11), according to many, refers to ordinary meals and not to the Lord's Supper, although that too would be forbidden. The difficulty is that Jesus ate with sinners and Paul, in 10:27, allows one to accept invitations to eat in heathen homes. The answer may be in a comparison of "not to keep company" and "not to eat." The former may denote regular intercourse and the latter not so. Without numerous hotels, private hospitality was important. The main theme remains: There is to be no close fellowship with one who claims to be a Christian, but whose life belies that claim.

Paul claims no authority to judge sinners or those outside the Christian community. But the Church must guard and watch those inside the Church. God will judge those outside[47] the Church. The Corinthians' indifference toward impurity must be resolved. Verse 12 points to their responsibility and verse 13 limits that responsibility.

The injunction is to remove the unrepentant offender because he is within the fold; he must be left to God's judgment. The purpose of this is to warn sinners of judgment and point them to the grace of God. But the injunction rises to the greater principle that the Church must continually examine itself and keep itself from all unrighteousness for Christ's sake for it belongs to Him.

C. The Nature and Evil of Lawsuits (6:1-11)

These two problems, the one just discussed and this one, are

47

connected by a spirit of greed and a lack of church discipline. Again the problem is discussed without preamble. Paul opposes the taking of difficulties between Christians before pagan courts. To do so is a bad example and shows immaturity. "Dare any of you" includes everyone and indicates immorality, immaturity, immodesty, audacity, and shamelessness. Generally, as we see from Romans 13, Paul's opinion of pagan magistrates is favorable. But here we are carried back to the arguments on wisdom and foolishness and reminded that the Corinthians cannot settle disputes because they do not heed the revelation of God to them.

"Not before the saints" (v. 1) indicates that it is not forbidden to seek justice. Law and order and an honest court are blessings from God. But the Corinthians were seeking the wrong advice and disputing petty matters. Paul never used the courts to accuse his injurers, but in defense of his work.[48]

Paul thinks these readers should know already (vv. 2, 3) that the saints will participate with Christ in judging the world. They will applaud His actions and just decisions. Brought into this circle by "world" and "angels," seem to be intelligent beings everywhere. Paul intends to establish a dignity, privilege, and association beyond the idea even of Christian magistrates. It is a picture of Christ and His saints in session, with the world brought in before them. With this position awaiting, are you unable, Paul asks, to handle petty matters among yourselves? Can you not form a "court" to settle your own disputes? The church had forgotten its glory and the honor of God. This was an insult to God's ability to impart wisdom and ability in Christ. "Matters" actually denotes the rules and means of judging and thus comes to be understood of the court itself.

Paul adds without explanation that the Church will judge angels (v. 3). This is discussed elsewhere in such passages as 2 Peter 2:4; Jude 6; and Revelation 20:10, but details are not included there either. Therefore, a discussion of the details would only be conjecture and unnecessary at this point. Paul's purpose is to pick something lofty and beyond this world. The Church would judge these. Why could it not handle smaller, less exalted affairs?

Verse 4 is actually a question intended to gain a negative answer. The unwise, weak, immature man is not to be the judge.

That would be foolish. But that is exactly what the Corinthians were allowing. By placing their cases before pagan judges, these men, who were less than the least in the Church, had become their judges. How foolish indeed!

To the further shame of the church, they had not even considered the idea of finding a wise man in their own midst to settle judiciary disputes. An arbiter was needed. There is a sting here because the Corinthians considered themselves wise.

Verse 6 answers verse 5 as we already have. Brothers fight; wisdom is lacking; evil rules the day. It is absurd that brothers should dispute like this. Love is not present. Faith is not being built. So they could not really call themselves brothers. Paul points them to a proper answer and attitude, for at the base of their problem is a motivating attitude that is wrong.

This litigation is soundly denounced (v. 7). "Fault" is properly "defeat" or loss.[49] While lawsuits are not branded as sinful, the nature and boasting behind them proved the Corinthians were defeated Christians. The defeat is proven by the lawsuits. Paul offers a solution and establishes the proper attitude for a Christian. We must serve our other brethren.[50] Paul's aim is to show that seeking justice, particularly on external things, is not the highest goal, but the rule of love. By this statement Paul reveals the Corinthians' lack of understanding and maturity in Christian principles.

Paul points out the hate, self-righteousness, and jealousy in their midst (v. 8). They were doing the wrong to others. They were defrauding their own brothers in Christ. They were not ready to suffer wrong; they were committing wrong. The duty and the fact were leagues apart.

Lumped with the misconduct of the Corinthians are other evidences of unrighteousness (vv. 9, 10), all of which will keep a man from the kingdom of God. The Corinthians had committed sins typical of the unrighteous. Paul does not suggest his readers had committed all the sins listed, but he does suggest that by their sin they had joined this unrighteous company. They thought themselves kings (4:8), but they ran the risk of being outside God's kingdom.

The list includes "fornicators," which involves all trespassers of the seventh commandment; the "effeminate" and "abusers of themselves with men" designate passive and active homosexuals respectively;[51] "idolaters" violate the first commandment; "adulterers" violate the seventh commandment, and in particular the marriage bed; "thieves" is a general description for robbers or thieves; the "covetous" include those who always lust after someone else's possessions, although they may not steal; "drunkards" consume alcoholic beverages to excess; "revilers" are those who abuse others; and "extortioners" suggests taking by force, violently. Such as do these things have no part in the kingdom of God and the Corinthians are in danger of placing themselves there. It might be added that the list seems to fall into the rough categories of sins against self and sins against others.

Before their conversion some of these Corinthians were members of this group (v. 11). The contrast is strong between then and now. Their lives have been changed. "Washed" carries the force of "you go yourselves washed." Some see a reference to water baptism. Others suggest the washing of Revelation 1:5. The tense is past; the aorist referring to a decisive action. "Sanctified" is in the same tense. They were set apart, perhaps referring to consecration. "Justified" is also an aorist and looks back to the time of their acceptance as righteous before God. This legal term was used by Paul for the act whereby God, on the basis of Christ's atoning death, declares sinners just and accepted. One question must be asked: Why does justification follow sanctification, when that is not the normal order? Paul may have felt that sanctification needed special stress because of the character implicit in such a process of grace.

"In" indicates both the sphere and ground of these actions. Note the full name which suggests Christ in all His relationships. Where He rules He gives His benefits to rely upon. "The Spirit of our God" points to the source of this changing, keeping power in these relationships, and "our God" denotes the same God who sent His Son and stands in opposition to the gods the Corinthians once served.

D. The Consecration of the Body (6:12-20)

Paul is now reaching his conclusion on this portion on social obligation and morality and the wrong attitudes of the Corinthians. He concludes his position by reminding them the body belongs to Christ.

"All things are lawful" (v. 1) appears to have been a common saying in this church. A principle of Christian liberty is expounded by Paul. He may do these things, but it is not a "must" situation. Certain limitations to this statement are made, but the truth of this statement stands because it deals with what is possible, but not necessarily best. That "all things" cannot be taken in an absolute sense is proven by the natural exclusion of murder, robbery, and other such prohibited acts. Paul's intent is to lead the readers to admit the truth of verse 12 and then, as he adds to this, they will be forced to admit their wrong (see v. 18). The permission for the statements of verse 12 is found in the standing of the Christian in Christ. If he is free to do all things, he is still not free to sin. The limitations are set by consequences and expediency.

Second, being brought under the wrong power would limit the opening statement of verse 12. The Corinthians thought they were free, but by their actions of fornication, etc., they had been brought under the power of sin.[52] By so doing, they had lost their liberty. Above all, the Christian must remain subject to God and to God alone. This verse gives the self-regarding rule and 10:23-33 gives the other-regarding rule of Christian temperance in the use of lawful things.[53] The Christian shares the authority of Christ, but that is not an allowance to do all things, even if the right is there.

The body has an express purpose (vv. 13, 14). It may well be the Corinthians had placed fornication on a morally indifferent level, arguing that the presence of bodily appetites was enough reason to gratify them. Perhaps they considered body and soul separate, and since the body was to be done away with, it made little difference what it did. Paul quickly cuts through this knot.

Paul admits natural appetites, but relegates them to a particular sphere. They are passing or transient. In due time God will do away with them or render them inoperative. But the body is not to be so done away with. Nor is fornication or any such impurity transient. It has a very permanent effect. Likewise, the connection is not between body and fornication (as between meats and belly), but between the body and the Lord. "God did not design the body for fornication as He did the belly for food."[54]

51

"Body" in Paul's thinking is the whole personality and being, as meant for God. The value of the body is then increased. It is to be treated with honor and care for it is for the Lord. "The Lord for the body" refers to the need of the body for the Lord. He must run and regulate it or else it fails to fulfill its proper function.

The potential of the body must be seen. As the Father raised Christ, so shall He raise us by His power (see chapter 15). The emphasis is on the importance of the body. The destiny of "belly" and "meats" is destruction. The destiny of the body is the resurrection and eternal life in Christ. This puts the body on a high plane indeed!

Paul has said the body is the Lord's and cannot function properly without Him, but he makes the union more intimate by establishing our membership with Christ as prohibitive to impurity (vv. 15-17). Paul asks a question intended to have a negative answer: Shall I take the members of Christ away and make them members of a prostitute or submit them to sin? Absolutely not! God forbid![55] This would involve deliberate alienation and defilement. Moral and spiritual ruin was caused by such actions; yet some dared to hold them as blameless as eating. How foolish!

This establishes a very intimate and binding relationship between Christ and the Body. As the Church is the body of Christ, so the various persons in the Church are members of Christ. As mentioned in verse 20, this is a complete and absolute union.

On the other hand, joining to a harlot is also a complex union for it involves physical, mental, and spiritual aspects (v. 16). One unit is formed. Paul reminds his readers of such passages as Genesis 2:24; Matthew 19:5; and Mark 10:8. The harlot is associated with evil and thus by this illicit union the union with Christ is damaged or even broken.

On the other hand, a proper relationship with Christ forms a total relationship that affects every avenue of the individual (v. 17). It is a proven fact that mind affects body and spirit and vice versa. This second potential relationship is on a far higher plane than the first. A man joined to a harlot descends to her filthiness. A man joined to Christ ascends to heavenly places. Our thoughts, desires, and actions become one with His in a mystical, wondrous union.[56]

Paul reaches a conclusion (vv. 18-20). It is based on what has preceded. "Flee fornication." Recall the story of Joseph at Potiphar's house. Some sins we have to stand up to and fight, but the answer to this one is flight. The sexual drive is very strong and we must guard against striking a spark in the passions that would lead to such sin. Every other sin, while affecting the body, does not wreak the devastation on it this one does, for this aims only at the satisfaction of lust. God's chosen possession dare not be defiled by such sacrilege. This sin goes against the very nature and purpose of the body. It becomes a self-violation. It demands the participation of the whole body, for it stems from the heart, the springs of being.[57] The temple of Aphrodite may have condoned it, but not the temple of God.

For the third time in this section Paul turns to a fact the readers should know: "Know ye not. . . ." The body is the temple of the Holy Spirit. Filth has no part there. Paul referred to the whole Christian church in 3:16, 17; here he refers to the individual member in the body of Christ. The Holy Spirit, sent from God, abides within and purifies the temple. But we as priests have a part in it also. This temple was bought by God through the blood of His Son Jesus and is now possessed by Him. The result is that this shrine is owned and possessed by the Holy Spirit. The temple does not draw dignity, honor, or purity from itself, but from the One who inhabits it—God.

The basis for verse 19, as already indicated, is: "You were bought with a price" (v. 20, *RSV*). The verb is an aorist and points to a single decisive action in time past. It reminds us of a custom of Paul's day. A slave could save the price of his freedom, pay it into the temple treasury, and be purchased by the god. Men called him free, but technically he was the slave of the god.[58]

Having been bought by Christ, it should be our single constant goal to glorify God. Here that principle applies directly to the body.[59] There is an urgency about this last command to glorify God. There must be no delay in obeying.

53

IV

Marriage
and
Celibacy
(7:1-40)

A. The Normalcy of Marriage (7:1-7)

˙ Some general comments about this section must be made as we begin to consider it. This subject matter has often caused controversy; partly because some reject its teachings, about which we can do little; and partly because some misunderstand what Paul says. The latter group may be spoken to by a clear discussion of the context. Further, this section was written in response to questions from the Corinthians themselves. This seems to be suggested throughout the letter by the phrase, "Now concerning. . . ." It is also important that we note the "good" of verse 1. This denotes a commendable, not a commanded, attitude and refers to sexual relationships within marriage, as we gather from "touch a woman." The question is whether or not one should marry. In verse 32 Paul will give his major reason for celibacy.

Clearly Paul wants the virtues of marriage understood. He is aware of the low moral tide in Corinth and of the dangers of fornication, as has just been discussed. Marriage is an antidote to perversion and lust. A particularly strong type of marriage is meant. "Each man" (v. 2, *NEB*) suggests a monogamous marriage, which is a commandment according to "Let . . . have. . . ." This is referred first to the man, then to the woman. This second verse also restricts verse 1, for the latter is only a restriction, not a universal rule. Paul is not downgrading marriage; he is replying within the context of a historical setting and problem. Therefore, the emphasis is on the absence of sin.

The marriage bond includes certain obligations (vv. 3-5). Both the husband and the wife have certain duties to their mate. Each partner has certain rights; they should be respected. This is a mark against the one-sidedness of Jewish marriage where the woman was often considered an animal. She also has her place and rights. This is reinforced by the use of "due" (v. 3), which involves the idea of a debt or what is owed.

It seems a fair deduction that some Corinthians advocated total sexual abstinence in marriage for one reason or the other. This is wrong, for it would involve needless temptation and dangerous sins could creep in. The husband and wife have some authority over each other. A mutual surrender is involved. Thus the husband, for example, cannot do alone what he pleases with his body. The wife has rights and privileges, and vice versa. In view of the widespread exaltation of celibacy, Paul's statements on the indispensability of the sex act in marriage are noteworthy.

Verse 5 then states the rule in marriage. What was stated positively in verse 3 is now stated negatively. Paul covers all points. Do not defraud your mate, for he (she) has certain rights over your body. Paul approves separation from sexual intercourse only under certain conditions. It must involve mutual consent; therefore, it is not really separation. It must be only for a limited time; a fixed agreed-upon time. It must have a definite purpose: to give oneself to prayer.[60] The Greek carries the article with it, indicating a specific prayer. Married life may place such demands on a person that such specific prayer cannot be maintained. This is not right. At such times, under the conditions already stated, abstinence would be best.[61]

Paul adds a more general admonition which is the real reason he has written this. It involves Satan's temptation of the Christian. Satan watches to trap every Christian. Man is built with a desire to express himself in a sexual manner. This expression is proper in marriage. But Satan tempts people by urging them to express themselves in an illicit manner, such as fornication. And the temptation to "incontinence" is stronger if such matters are not properly handled in the marriage arrangement.

In verse 6 Paul speaks "this by permission."[62] Commandment is the opposite of concession. Paul does not command Christians to marry. But on the other hand, neither does he reluctantly admit the right to marry. Every Christian has the right to marry, but this does not mean exercising this right is necessary. Ordinary situations would, however, suggest this.

The exception is found in a man like Paul himself (v. 7). The Corinthians knew what and who he was. The indication is that Paul was unmarried at this time. Whether he was ever married is a much more difficult question. His ability, nonetheless, to remain unmarried and refrain from fornication was due to a special ability and gift from God. It aided in the spread of the gospel.

Paul does not lift himself above any other Christian. God gives as He chooses, in His will and wisdom.[63] Paul's intention is that the gospel be preached with great power and that nothing interfere with it whether one is married or single. Purity and power with God are his goals. Paul may prefer the celibate state, but he recognizes that both marriage and celibacy are God-given orders; therefore, each man must recognize God's gifts to him and God's will for him.

B. The Marriage Question Related to Various Groups/Situations (7:8-24) (Abide in One's Calling)

Having established basic principles regarding marriage, Paul now applies these to individual situations. He speaks first to the unmarried and widows (vv. 8, 9). "Unmarried" probably refers to unmarried men,[64] and the widows are especially mentioned because of their dependence and vulnerability. Again the base of verse 1 is seen. It is good for them to remain as they are— unmarried; just as Paul is at this time.

Once more, however, a restriction appears (v. 9). The controlling rule depends on the gift of continence, which is a God-determined gift. Otherwise, "Let them marry" appears as a command not as permission. It is better to marry than to continually burn with sexual desire. If this is the case there is no advantage to celibacy. Paul did not regard the suppression of sexual desire as meritorious in itself. There had to be a greater purpose. "To burn" is in the present, indicating a continuous urge, while the answer lies in the single definite act of marriage. The principle is that whatever is morally better, within God's call, should be the determining factor.

Paul then turns his attention to those who are married and Christians (vv. 10, 11). It must be repeated that here both partners appear as Christians. This time Paul gives his advice on the basis of a direct command of the Lord. He has appealed to the words of Christ before[65]; here the reference is probably Matthew 5:32; 19:3-9; Mark 10:11, 12. Such a reference is necessary lest his readers think that being married is also only "good." And such a reference will throw tremendous weight behind what he says.

Paul mentions the wife first, thus emphasizing her place. In the Gospel passages referred to, Christ was speaking primarily to Jews; in such a society the husband put away his wife, but the wife did not leave. But in Corinth women were much more liberated. Paul wants it understood that neither partner has the right to leave.[66] He has also just been speaking to women who are widows, and it may be his readers had asked if a woman was allowed to leave.

If a woman does depart, however, one of two things should happen. Paul is not approving divorce here, but saying if it happens in spite of everything done to prevent it, the wife must remain alone or be reconciled to her husband. He offers no other alternatives. Reconciliation would probably have to begin with the party who did the departing or divorcing. God made one husband for one wife, etc., and anything contrary in this setting is breaking Christ's command.

Similarly the husband cannot separate from the wife. The verb is different but the result is the same. Paul does not mention fornication here or its effects, as Jesus does in Matthew, probably because of the specific nature of the question.

In verse 12 Paul begins his application of the principles already cited to what he terms the "rest," which specifically involves various mixed marriage relationships. By "mixed" we mean situations where an unbeliever and a believer are married. It expressly concerns a situation where the unbeliever is willing to continue the marriage relationship. It also apparently refers to those who after marriage become Christians; one partner becomes a believer. There is no ground for a Christian marrying a non-Christian in order to win him to the Lord.[67]

Paul remarks, ". . . speak I, not the Lord." Why? This is not contrary to what the Lord would have ordered. Verse 10 carried an express command of Christ. Here Paul does not have such words of Christ and thus makes the situation clear. He is, nevertheless, speaking by divine permission and authority and under the inspiration of the Holy Spirit. Paul ends this chapter by assuring his readers that he believes he has the Spirit of the Lord in these matters. Moffatt points out that Paul's careful distinction here opposes those who maintain that the Early Church made a habit of producing needed sayings and ascribing them to Christ.[68]

Some Corinthians thought it was necessary to divorce a mate when the latter remained pagan. The idea was that such pagan contact would defile the new Christian. But "to be content" renders this idea unnecessary and even forbidden. The outcome depends on the attitude of the pagan partner. In verse 13 Paul repeats the principles of verse 12 to the wife.

Paul continues by offering an explanation for what he has said (v. 14). He refers to a sanctifying influence, which pertains to a certain relation to God, not moral uprightness. It does not mean the unbeliever is holy before God in Christ. He uses the word in the same sense in 1 Timothy 4:5. The believer is set apart to God. His relation to God is not diminished because before believing he married an unbeliever. Rather, the believer exerts an influence on the unbelieving partner and the home. If they live together in love, the unbeliever shows externally that he belongs with believers. Being one flesh with the believer is very important for the unbeliever.[69] Such scriptural blessings from a fellowship with God also extend to others, not just to immediate recipients.[70]

The children of such a union also serve as examples. If a sanctifying influence did not carry over to the family, the children could not be brought into contact with divinity. Until the age when a child is able to make a personal decision in the matter, his life is sheltered by the faith of his parents. Indeed, the believing partner exerts a holy, sanctifying influence on the whole family.

But the unbeliever may choose to not remain with the believing partner (v. 15). The fact that the unbeliever is the subject places the full burden of separation on his shoulders.[71] If the unbeliever chooses not to abide willingly and peacefully with the believer but to depart, he should be allowed to go. In such cases the believer is not under bondage. The question of remarriage does not technically appear here. On the basis of verse 11, it would seem that for the divorced to remain unmarried is the safer. It is, in fact, most improbable that Paul would contradict a command of Christ; He allowed divorce only on the ground of unfaithfulness. Many feel, however, that if the unbeliever forms a new union then the exception of Matthew 5:32 comes into play and the divorced believer may remarry a believer.

The Christian spouse now forsaken is free from the former yoke (vv. 15, 16). What should the guiding pursuit be? Peace. The work of Christ resulted in peace with God as Romans 5:1 tells us. This causes internal peace to prevail throughout the whole life.[72] Nothing should be allowed to disturb that peace. But here we approach two difficult views as to verses 15, 16. One view would read like this: "If this peace would be disturbed by the continuation of a mixed marriage, then the yoke of bondage need not be shouldered but divorce is permissible."[73] Some would argue that the marriage should be preserved because the unbelieving partner might be saved. This is uncertain and marriage is more than a tool of evangelism. Some conflict causes tension and frustration and the aim is peace. Under certain circumstances then this view supports separation.

The other view reads like this: The Christian spouse who has been forsaken is free from the former yoke, but such freedom is undesirable for two reasons: (1) there is the possibility of saving the unbeliever, and (2) peace is better than disruption. By a contrastive δέ Paul reverts to the prevailing thought that marriage ties once formed should in every possible way be maintained. In other words, this reads: "How do you know you will not save" the unbelieving spouse? This opposes all separation. This latter view is supported by the following arguments: Grammatical considerations appear balanced and therefore the tenor of the previous context shows Paul's meaning; the first view reads between the lines; these readers needed reasons for not divorcing, not the opposite; to discourage the hope of someone's salvation seems unlike the apostle Paul.[74]

The first view, however, seems the stronger; and this without referring to the fact that most modern exegetes accept it. All grammatical considerations do not seem equal. The argument hinges on the εἰ which the latter view interprets "that . . . not" and turns to an English idiom (as though it were, "How do you know? It may be you will save . . ."). This is forced. It would appear better for literal translation to go with "whether" (if). Salvation involves a personal decision. Paul does not exclude the unbeliever's salvation at any time here. The emphasis is on the believer and maintaining inner peace. Marriage is not merely evangelism; it is an intimate, deep, lasting relationship that joins body as well as spirit. Ultimately, a relationship with God is individual and must take priority. God has ordained certain channels of authority, but the most important is still between God and the individual.

It must be emphasized that we are not advocating divorce or separation. Paul lists certain qualifications here and this is the last possible move after all steps have been taken to maintain the relationship under God, and after the conscience has been totally absolved of blame. The situation is specifically limited and again the unbeliever must initiate the action.

With the summation in verse 17 Paul both reminds us of what he has been saying and allows an enlargement of this basic principle to apply to all of life in covering both the major political and the major social divisions of the day. One must remain in one's calling. In Thessalonica the coming of Christianity had created a conflict with domestic relations so that they had abandoned daily work and thrown their support upon the church.[75] In Corinth the effect had been one of a disregard of self-esteem, self-worth, morality, and blessing. There had been a disregard for their station in life. Paul battles this wider tendency in the following.

God both calls and maintains. He distributes blessings and gifts. "But" *(KJV)* or "only" *(ASV)* puts it opposite the preceding as a standing rule. "Hath distributed" implies God's governing influence in everyone's life both spiritually and naturally. Returning to the marriage relationship, it must be remembered that freedom for the Christian is not license. Opposed to liberty is the fact that the Christian has certain marital obligations, including the maintenance of one's present state as normal Christian practice. "Hath called" denotes that when God chooses, He expects one to live the life He sets before him, using the gifts He gives him. "Walk" is an oft-repeated word with Paul and here denotes a steady, continual progress. We must accept God's call and gifts, remain contentedly there, and bring glory to God.

This was not something Paul drew up especially for the Corinthians; he preached this in all the churches. The message was constant.

Paul then applies this principle to the racial, political distinction between circumcision and uncircumcision (vv. 18, 19). Paul says this is of the outer man and of no importance. The Jews demanded circumcision; otherwise, they were cut off from the blessings of God. The Gentiles, on the other hand, saw circumcision as the mark of a despised people. It was a sign of liberty when, as sometimes happened, a Jewish youth underwent surgery to remove the marks of circumcision, to better please the Greek culture within which he lived. One interesting example of this is found among certain young Jews in Jerusalem at the time of Antiochus Epiphanes, king of Syria (175-164 B.C.), who ruled Palestine and tried to abolish Jewish religion. Wishing to adopt the Greek ways of life and probably wishing to include the custom of engaging in athletic exercises naked as the Greeks did, these young Jews submitted to a surgical operation to conceal their circumcisions.[76]

But whether or not there were those at Corinth who were trying to conceal their Jewish origin is difficult to say. It is more likely there were those who thought circumcision necessary to more fully obey God. Nevertheless, Paul mentions both viewpoints regarding circumcision. This is to make a point. A man may find himself in various circumstances when he is called by the Lord. These outward circumstances, distinctions, and conditions are of no importance. The important thing is the commandments of God and keeping them. A man should not worry over or seek to change his circumstances; he should not seek to be what he is not. Rather, he should obey the moral law of God. No amount of ritual may be placed alongside this. The important thing is that a man is called and that he abides in and walks according to his vocation.

For emphasis, Paul reiterates what he has said in verse 17 (v. 20). Despite outward circumstances, each man should individually remain in his calling to be a Christian. He is ever to be the representative of Jesus Christ. "Calling" notes the act; "abide" notes its continuance. The principle therefore is perpetual.

After this Paul applies this principle to the great social distinction of his day (v. 21); that of slaves and free men. Slaves in the Corinthian church may have supposed their first concern to be natural freedom. But, while Paul did not necessarily believe in slavery, his first aim was not social revolution, but spiritual reformation. It was possible, Paul preached, to be a Christian in any situation.

And if the slave had an opportunity to be free, Paul says to use it. What does he mean by this? Most conclude that Paul is supporting either continued slavery or using acquired freedom. The second seems the most logical and the best supported by arguments. Those who support the idea of remaining in slavery have an exaggerated sense of verses 20 and 24, which do not condemn change per se but because it compromises Christian faith and standing. "Freedom" would seem to be the most natural object of "rather use"; also the sense of "using" in verse 31 would support this. Verses 15 and 23 give us some idea of Paul's concept of freedom, which would seem to suggest that if the offer were made, freedom should be accepted. Also against maintaining slavery is the aorist imperative which more naturally signifies the beginning of a new "use." Further, with Paul's views of the complications of marriage to Christian service, it is difficult to suppose he had different views concerning slavery.[77]

But the slave is not to worry. He has been called by Christ. The world does not determine a man's position, God does. In Christ all are equal. The necessary condition is our affection for and relationship to the Lord.

With verse 23 Paul returns to his basis of 6:20. Believers have been bought with the blood of Jesus Christ. This is a ground to prompt obedience to Christ and remaining in the call to His service. One may be a slave, but he is free from sin and guilt. The other may be free, but he is bound to obedience and service to Christ (v. 22). Therefore, they dare not become real slaves of men. In the pursuit of wisdom, for example, these readers must seek God's truth, not some man's philosophy or manner of presenting the gospel. They dare not pursue worldly distinctions or merely natural freedom. Sometimes it is easy to accept unquestioningly what others lay down, and thus display the mentality of a slave. A certain freedom of mind and spirit to Christ is necessary for the Christian.

Finally in verse 24, Paul repeats the principle of this section. A man is to serve God where he is until God calls somewhere else. "Was called" is an aorist, pointing back to the time of God's call; "therein abide" is present continuous, indicating continuity.[78] And the ever-present God, who is also faithful, is who we are to abide with; not in resignation at all costs, but in loving, contented, happy, active service. The will and pleasure of God must first be consulted in every change and work. "Abide with God."

C. Advantages in the Unmarried State (7:25-40)

"Now concerning" indicates yet another matter on which the Corinthians had submitted written questions (v. 25). "Virgins" probably refers to women (and includes the question of daughters at home and the father's responsibility). As before where there are no specific commandments or words of Christ, the position is made clear. There is no distinction here between rule and advice. "Judgment" does not leave the case open to doubt or uncertainty. What is said is based on the risen Christ's mercy to Paul. It points out Paul's significance while giving the glory to God. When Paul gave this advice it was done in faithfulness to the Lord; it must, therefore, be pleasing to Him. It could thus be trusted. God's grace had made Paul a trustworthy servant and apostle.

This "judgment" is begun then in verse 26. "I think" *(RSV)* should be understood in the same sense as "judgment" in the previous verse. It suggests definite opinion. Paul stresses two things: It is a good thing to be a virgin because of the present need, and it is a good thing in itself. The "present distress" is a general reference to the needs of all Christians. The context includes descriptions like "tribulation in the flesh" (v. 28, *ASV*), "time is short" (v. 29), and "fashion of this world passeth away" (v. 31). The consequences of sin are seen. The Christian, whether married or unmarried, was caught in a struggle and pressure. What that pressure really consisted of cannot be traced. But the reference is to unusually difficult circumstances. In such trouble the advice is for men (or women) to remain as they are.[79]

He enlarges on what he means. The moment Paul recommends remaining single under the "present distress," he has to answer questions concerning those already married (vv. 27, 28). Should they separate? The answer is no. And such unity is a command of the Lord (v. 10). The application here is to men. "Art thou loosed" may mean simply unmarried.

Verse 28 shows the force of the end of verse 27. It is made clear first to men then to virgins that marriage is not a sin. Perhaps some Corinthians had misinterpreted Paul's words and had this view of marriage. Paul makes no absolute prohibitions concerning marriage. Marriage may involve distress, but not immorality.

There are various views on "tribulation in the flesh" (v. 28, *ASV*). Some claim a reference to bodily difficulties of married women. But this appears too limited, and "such" is masculine, embracing more than married women. Some see a reference to the problems created by agitation against the gospel, which are increased by a man's regard for his wife and children. Such blessings enrich a man's life, but mishaps to them are more difficult to handle. Photius indicated: "More easily and with small distress shall we endure if we have no wives and children to carry along with us in persecutions and countless miseries." Sometimes a decision must be made between God and family. It is Paul's intention in wisdom and love to spare them these difficulties; to aid and help rather than adding pressure. Hence Paul's advice.

Certain related items must be included in this context to cover his theme (vv. 29-31). By "brethren" Paul addresses the whole congregation with this important, loving message. Paul will speak to attitude and conduct. In "the time is shortened" *(ASV)* some see a reference to the second advent; others to a crisis in Corinth. We do live between the descent of the Holy Spirit and the return of Jesus Christ. The Second Coming demands the end of all things and hastens us toward that end.[80] For that reason our lives should be directed toward eternal events. But this does not mean Paul was certain of the coming of the Lord in his own lifetime. He merely lived expectantly, while working all the time and preparing for tomorrow. "Henceforth" (v. 29, *ASV*) carries the idea that there remains only one thing necessary; the eye must be directed toward heaven.

From this point Paul lists five examples of the Christian's freedom from the world of transience. Notice that each item can be connected with the married state. "As though they had none" (v. 29) is not an exhortation to marital neglect, but an indication that marriage must be kept in proper perspective. Every Christian is going to weep, rejoice, and buy (v. 30) as he shares in the events of his world and time. But these are not to be the determinants in the character of the Christian. In each situation the heart must be directed heavenward. The Christian is not acquiring lasting possessions here. The world has merely the passing fashion of the theater or stage. As J. H. Newman wrote: "Then what this world to thee, my heart? Its gifts nor feed thee nor can bless. Thou hast no owner's part in all its fleetingness."[81]

The addition and summary of verse 31 appears with an air of detachment. "Using it to the full" *(ASV)* indicates a man who uses the world in that manner and then has nothing left when the world passes. Rather it should be as the song tells us, "This world is not my home, I'm just passing through." For the world has a transitory nature and form and it will pass away. This is inevitable. This world has been judged and stands condemned. A present action is involved in this "passing away." What a solemn warning must be received from this comment. Attachments in this world will pass away; they will not last.

Instead of fixing transitory values on the world, Paul desires unworried service for the Lord (vv. 32-34). He wishes that his friends be free from care and unnecessary pressure. This care would distract from perfect service toward God. The unmarried man does not have such "cares" or hindrances to serving the Lord as marriage offers; thus, Paul's preference for celibacy. He longs to see undistracted service for the Lord.

The cares of the married and the "freedom" of the single are further compared. Paul relates that the married man has some concern for "the things of the world" *(ASV)*. This does not denote "worldliness" or sin. It is rather a note that the married man has family interests and obligations. The married man must face the question of "how he may please his wife," which is a direct parallel with "how he may please the Lord" (v. 32).[82] Such a man is divided in interest and purpose between God and wife.

The same difference that exists between married and unmarried men is found between married and unmarried women. The

66

unmarried can more fully concentrate on the things of God. The unmarried can have a singleness of purpose regarding consecration and the pursuit of the holy. This does not make the virgin any more righteous than the wife. But the wife must take into account the needs of her husband and so her consecration is "modified" by her dual purpose. Thus Paul is stressing one great difference: the unmarried has one set of cares, the married two. Paul is not stressing individual cases. These are made distinct. That is enough.

Paul's purpose is not to place undue restraints or absolutes on his readers (v. 35). Rather his advice is for the purpose of gaining their best, undistracted service to the Lord. Paul speaks of spiritual advantage. This third time we are advised that Paul is writing for the welfare of his readers. Paul does not wish to wrap[83] his readers in celibacy, but only to refer them to what is honorable and fit for the Lord. There is a parallel with Martha in Luke 10:38-42.

Again Paul returns to the question of marriage and virgins specifically (vv. 36-38). His statements on celibacy are qualified by his indication that marriage is nevertheless not to be despised. At this point, some differences of opinion must be noted. One view is that "man" (v. 36) is a general term for parent or guardian. "Behaveth himself unseemly" *(ASV)* means dishonorable treatment; in this case failing to provide for her marriage. To withhold marriage from a girl of marriageable age who was anxious to marry, would have been dangerous, especially in first-century Corinth. "If she pass the flower of her age" is a very unusual expression. It seems to mean "if she pass the stage of being fully developed"; in other words, at or past an age when marriage is most natural. "Need" may refer to either the lack of the gift of continence, or a moral obligation. The guardian or parent may then do as he pleases. He may "let them marry." While this seems the best view, there are two major objections: one is that "his virgin" is not a common expression for "his daughter" (however, it does occur); and, second, "let them marry" is most naturally taken as referring to the man and virgin spoken of earlier in the verse. (But it can refer to the daughter and her suitor.)

A second view is that the case is one of a man and his betrothed. The pair had first agreed to remain celibate. Paul explains that there is no sin if they change their minds and marry. There are several strong objections to this view, however: (1) Why should people become engaged if they do not intend to be "united" in marriage sexually? (2) It is difficult to put meaning into "behaveth himself unseemly" with this view; and, (3) "His virgin" is a strange designation for a man's fiancee.

There is a third view that suggests that Paul is indicating "spiritual marriage," whereby some went through a marriage form, but lived as brother and sister. They abstained from sexual intercourse. Thus Paul would be giving permission to such to marry and consummate the marriage in physical union if the strain was too great. The objections to this view are even more obvious: (1) in verse 5, Paul regards the withholding of sexual relations by married partners as fraudulent; (2) the first known record of such action is at the end of the second century; and, (3) it is necessary to adopt an unnatural rendering of "giveth . . . in marriage" in verse 38.[84]

But there are circumstances which may allow the virgin to be "kept" from marriage (v. 37). This includes the man remaining unchanged and not thinking he is behaving unseemly. There must be "no necessity"; probably sexual urge.[85] If he controls his own will, unlike a slave, he can prevent the marriage. In such cases the man who has determined to keep his virgin unmarried shall do well.[86]

Marriage is proper, not sinful, and the father does well in giving his daughter in marriage. But Paul indicates his own preference by stating that the man who refrains does better (v. 38). Again the view is heavenly not earthly. And again there is a consideration of the gifts of God in the matter. Neither is wrong, but a choice is involved as to which will bring the greatest service to the Lord.

In concluding his statements (vv. 39, 40) Paul advises regarding widows and remarriage. With these words Paul really disposes of the question of marriage, not as related to maidens only, but also to others. A wife is obligated as long as her husband lives. If the husband should die, the woman is free to marry according to her choice and will, with one exception. Her new spouse must be a believer, one "in the Lord." This would also involve seeking the Lord's will and good pleasure in the matter.

But Paul is of the opinion that she would be happier if she remained a widow. She would be, in particular, happier religiously, in her undisturbed devotion to the Lord. And Paul concludes that in these matters he has not merely been bending to personal bias, but has been advised by the Spirit of God, in his position as a called apostle. He voices not merely private opinion, but that which comes from divine enablement.

V

Liberty
and
Love
(8:1 to 11:1)

A. The Conscience of Liberty

1. The Clear Conscience of Love (8:1-13)

As we begin this new section some words of introduction must be offered. Some things are always approved as right for the Christian; others are considered as universally wrong and condemned. But there is a third group that are considered right by some, but wrong by others; thus they become questions of conscience. Such at Corinth was the eating of meat that had been sacrificed to idols. The question was a serious one for the Corinthian Christians because they were continually confronted with it. Such meat was used at all the social occasions; it was on sale in all the regular public markets and could appear on the table of a host or friend.

Paul therefore sets forth certain principles, which are valid and of use to this very day. Paul refers to these same problems in 1 Corinthians 6:12 and Romans 14:1 to 15:13. But these three chapters carry the fullest treatment of the subject.

"Now concerning" (v. 1, *ASV*) calls to our attention again a problem the Corinthians had referred to Paul in a previous letter. "Things sacrificed to idols" *(ASV)* stands out as a clear caption of what is to follow, and with "we know . . . all have knowledge" Paul places himself in the situation. And here Paul begins to teach his readers. Knowledge was of great value to the Corinthians and Paul agrees with the importance and exercise of knowledge. But the Corinthians had the wrong starting point, for they were allowing the wrong things to guide their knowledge. The Corinthians tried to answer their problems with knowledge alone; Paul immediately makes it clear that knowledge must be tempered with a liberal dose of love.

To begin to prove his point, Paul contrasts knowledge and love. He reminds his readers that "knowledge puffeth up"; in other words, it can create pride, intellectual snobbery, and a "party spirit" which is opposed to the genuine Christian spirit. Love, on the other hand, "edifieth" or builds up. The great Corinthian flaw was their poverty of love. The Corinthians were in dire need of understanding just what built a mature, strong church. The verb *edifieth,* in actuality, refers to the putting up of buildings; Paul uses it here figuratively to mean the building of Christian character and the Christian church. Knowledge alone could destroy the church; love and knowledge together could build it. Edification is the natural outgrowth of love (Ephesians 4:15ff.; Matthew 22:37-40; 1 John 4:16-21).

The problem with knowledge alone is that it has limitations (v. 2). No matter how much a man thinks he knows, he still does not know fully or properly.[87] As Kay once put it: "Knowledge is proud that it has learnt so much. Wisdom is humble that it knows no more."[88] For the lack in knowledge, even when the content is correct, is the guiding manner and hand of love.

One might expect Paul to now remark, "But if any loves God, he has real knowledge." But Paul skims over the intermediate steps and ascends to what is really important. What really matters is not our knowledge but God's.[89] At this point, at least, Paul dare not ascribe anything to human acquisition. For to be known by God means to share in His grace; having first been recognized by Him.[90] Then proper knowledge, in the hand of love, is returned to us and we have a right foundation for our action.

With "concerning . . . idols" (v. 4) Paul returns to the immediate question. "We know" continues the thought from verse 1. This is typical of Paul's style of writing.

When Paul writes that "an idol is nothing,"[91] he is really saying it has no real place in the world; it has no power over the elements of nature. Rather, there is one God who controls earth and sky; the world is controlled by Him. This faith will rescue any Christian from superstition and fear. An idol is the product of man and thus has no real influence in the realm in which God Jehovah operates.

72

It is true (and this may be a quote from the Corinthians' letter to Paul) there are claims (v. 5) to the godship (deity) and lordship (dominion) of idols. In point of fact, there are literally multitudes of these claims. But by this very multitude there is a proven inadequacy on their part. For the fact remains that even in heathen circles there is only one true God.

On this hinge of one true God then Paul hangs an important argument (v. 6). Christians contrast sharply with idolaters: "yet [but] to us" *(ASV)*. "Father" denotes a special relationship as Creator and as spiritual Father, "of whom are all things" and "we [in] unto him" *(ASV)*. The universe and all else exists by Him. Therefore, we too are reserved for His purposes and glory. He will reap in "us" His glory, as a father would through his children. This relationship is possible through the "Lord Jesus Christ," who is here designated in all of His functions as Master, Mediator, and Friend. Thus, the universe is "of God through Christ" and we are "unto [for] him [God]; . . . [through] Christ" *(ASV)*.[92] Such faith leaves no place for false deities. The inference from such an argument is that the meat offered to these idols was unaffected because the sacrificial rites were hollow and powerless. This is absolutely true. But there is another consideration, as Paul will show.

"Howbeit" (v. 7) shows Paul is not in total agreement with the Corinthians' approach. They have left out a vital ingredient. This knowledge proclaimed in verse 6 is not present in every man. For Paul to say this does not contradict verse 1. These men may have knowledge on the subject, but their knowledge does not rid them of the consciousness that what they eat is sacrificial idol meat and that they are somehow connected with the idol.[93] "With conscience of the idol"[94] could refer to either a weakness of understanding or a force of habit, or both. The person then lives with a haunting sense that what he eats belongs to idols; he is associated with idols; he has sinned (note Romans 14:23). This weak conscience continues, being unable to discern clearly whether the act is right or wrong, but unable to remove the feeling of guilt and dread.

It is possible that in verse 8 Paul is once again referring to the letter the Corinthians had sent him; perhaps even quoting from it.[95] But he uses it to double advantage. Neither partaking nor abstaining will draw us to God or present us to Him. Food is too small and God too great to allow the former to determine our relationship to Him. Abstinence will not cast us from God as the weak might have been led to believe, and indulgence will not make anyone better as the proud might have wished.

But again this is not at the heart of the matter. For there follows (v. 9) a solemn warning concerning the assertion of one's personal rights. This can affect our standing with God. Love is essential in our relationship with God; therefore, it is essential in our relationship with the brethren. Love for the brethren demands that we reckon with the frailties of the weak. Meat in itself is a neutral item and may be refrained from for the good of another.[96]

To enlarge his point, Paul presents an illustration for his readers (vv. 10-12). He pictures the example of a knowledgeable, stronger Christian at a temple feast. A touch of bravado is even thrown in. He might be there from obligation or official ceremony, for such a happening in a pagan city would not occur apart from a meal in the temple. Or it might be the result of the general conduct of a Corinthian who considered idol meat as merely "ordinary." Here Paul censures it because of its effect on others. In 1 Corinthians 10:18-22, he will oppose it on its own account. The picture continues. A "weak" brother, as was possible in open feasts, observes the example. By a question (v. 10) Paul affirms that the weak brother is emboldened[97] to eat the idol meat. The result is the weak brother perishes or "is perishing"; he comes to sin. And what compounds this dismal picture is that this brother is one for whom Christ died. If Christ would die for him, what must the stronger brother be willing to do for him?

This sin enacted by the stronger brother has further complications. It is against the brethren, the church as a whole (v. 12), and it is the sin of "wounding" a weak conscience. A wound is inflicted; for this conscience is driven in a direction by example that it would not have taken on its own and where it is not allowed to go. The weak brother is not strong enough to participate, his conscience is defiled, and he sins.

And the final awful truth is that Christ is sinned against. He is robbed of the soul for which He died. There is little regard for Christ's work on the cross. What awful penalty must await such a destroyer!

74

With verse 13 Paul concludes this first point of his discussion. His direction is clear. Abstinence, under certain circumstances, is declared best. But a simple warning must be offered. Not just any situation demands such forbearance, for some go to an opposite extreme. Nonetheless, Paul will under no circumstances bear the awful burden of causing someone to stumble and sin; that must be prevented at all costs.[98] Actually Paul's statement is wider than some would think, for the word *meat* here in verse 13 is a general term relating to food, not just to idol meat. Paul is deeply involved in the issue; it is close to his heart for he uses the term *brother* four times in the last three verses. This problem touches all Christians. To protect, care for, and love the weaker brother Paul's abstinence would continue, if need be, "while the world standeth." This term involves the next age—evermore, forever, for eternity. Paul himself was willing to do this and the Corinthians had to follow his example as he followed Christ.

Paul's aim above all else is a mature Christian life. To that end he always moves; for that involves serving Christ to the best of one's being. In this chapter Paul recognizes that in Christianity there is a certain "freedom"; certain rights involved in knowledge. But again the guide in conduct is love: for God and man. And Paul determines in this area that there shall be no blemish on his record; he shall indeed have the clear conscience of love amidst liberty.

2. *The Example of Liberty in Conscience (9:1-14)*

After suggesting his own example, Paul begins to prove he has the kind of example that can be trusted and followed. In other words, he lives by the principles he sets down on questions of conscience.

With the question, "Am I not free?" (v. 1), to which Paul expects a positive reply, he is establishing that, like all Christians, he has certain undeniable Christian rights and privileges. Paul was not bound by the Old Testament Mosaic restrictions. In Christ he had freedom. The argument from chapter 8 is progressing.

The positive response to "Am I not an apostle"?[99] again indicates his privileges, this time in the special position of God's called apostle. He had seen "Jesus our Lord."[100] He had beheld the glorified Redeemer, probably on the Damascus Road. He is

75

therefore an apostle in the fullest sense. The use of "Jesus" alone is rare with Paul. He may be thinking again of the Damascus Road, or probably of the humanity of Christ.

Further, the apostle's work had borne fruit. The Corinthians were his "work in the Lord." The emphasis is yet on God. Therefore, the Corinthians ought to be the last to doubt Paul's apostleship because he was their spiritual father; they were living proof of the effectiveness of his work. They were, in fact, the "seal" (v. 2) of his apostleship. The seal was important in a day when many could not read. The mark stamped on clay or wax was first a mark of ownership, then a means of authentication.[101] Their existence as Christians proved his point for he had won them to Christ. This is not only a defense to Paul's critics; it also bears directly on the question of rights.

Thus Paul gives an answer to his examiners. "This" (v. 3) points to the two previous verses. It appears that Paul's apostleship, not the rights of apostleship in verse 4 and following, is what is under attack; thus, Paul defends this to make his argument accepted. Even if Paul's use of his rights had been criticized, it would have been much easier to accept if he were regarded as a true apostle.[102] If Paul had established his apostleship, the rights should be granted as well. However, because the point cannot be argued effectively on a grammatical basis, but only from a logical and contextual standpoint, the difference of opinion on this view is acute. Whatever one decides, the issue remains the same. Paul wishes to point out that all must be an example of love in liberty as he has been.

After all, Paul had the authority to "eat and to drink" (v. 4). It may be that Paul is reminding his friends that he has full rights, as in verse 1. But more probably Paul is speaking of this at the church's expense; in other words, of the right to maintenance. The interesting thing is that as Paul continues he does not include much wealth or great sums of money. He does expect to be able to "lead about a wife" (v. 5). But this particular question cannot be limited to marriage only. That would not have been argued. The question with its positive response leads to not only support for the apostle, but also leaves the implication that the wife too should be supported by the church. For support Paul points to the actions of other Christian teachers. The reference to "other apostles" indicates that a number were married. "Brethren of the Lord" in its most natural interpretation would refer to the children of Joseph and Mary. But this is difficult to ascertain. Certainly his readers knew what Paul meant. "Cephas" is picked for special mention because of his place in the eyes of these Corinthians. He was an outstanding apostle.

The questions continue; each anticipating a positive answer. Paul expects, along with Barnabas (who apparently also supported himself while spreading the gospel), to be able to "forbear working" (v. 6). The view again is to desist from supportive labor, from manual work, to spend full time spreading the gospel, and thus be maintained by the church.

Having defended his rights and privileges by the actions of other Christian teachers, Paul now turns to the custom of society (v. 7). Paul lists examples of the soldier, the vinedresser, and the shepherd. Like Christ before him, Paul found great power in these simple illustrations.[103] Each one mentioned had a different position and place in life: one was an employee, one an owner, and one (the shepherd), perhaps, a slave. But the common point is that each was fed from his occupation. He shared in the productiveness of his work.

Yet Paul wants it understood that he is not speaking from the standpoint of human wisdom only. Some might accuse him of this on the basis of his previous "natural" illustrations. So Paul proceeds a step farther. There is a link with divine truth and legal justice here. Paul expects a negative answer to the first question (v. 8) and an affirmative to the second. The "law" is regarded as authoritative. It is a (the) source of truth and right, and Paul uses it for Christian guidance.

The reference is to Deuteronomy 25:4 (v. 9). The "law of Moses" properly refers to the first five Books of the Old Testament. Whether it is intended to be so limited here is difficult to say. But the reference is to the ox who, while tramping the corn, shook the grain loose from its husk. After that the mixture was tossed in the air. The wind carried the lighter chaff away. Then the animal was allowed to eat some of the heavier grain which fell back to the floor. On this basis Paul asks, "Doth God take care for oxen?" The expected answer is, "No!" But this must be understood carefully. Paul does not mean God is indifferent to the needs of animals, but he is noting where the primary application is. What holds true for beasts of service must hold true in greater fact to God's servants. The quote applies first and foremost to preachers of the gospel (v. 10). God provides for the needs of the Christian laborer from the fruits of his labor; thus "plowing" and "threshing" should be done in hope and expectation.

Argument may also be made from the sense of natural justice (vv. 11, 12). The opening conditional clause of verse 11 implies that the condition had been fulfilled. The man who labors to produce the harvest is entitled to share in the proceeds. Paul had labored in the things of the Spirit; deep and wise. He was therefore entitled to material and bodily, not sinful, benefits. Considering the vast gulf between "spiritual" and "carnal," it is no wonder Paul could ask, "Is it a great thing?" and expect a negative answer. "Others" had exercised this right of maintenance and Paul does not begrudge them this; it is proper. But they had a lesser claim on the Corinthians than Paul, for he was their spiritual father.

But now the point is made. These rights which were theirs, they had not exercised. Rather they had "suffered"[104] for the gospel. It is not easy to support oneself and continue the heavy load of spreading the gospel. But this Paul and his co-workers had done. Some thought Paul had not made a claim to maintenance because he was an "inferior" apostle and recognized it. But Paul says it was that they "should [not] hinder the gospel of Christ."[105] Some would claim Paul was preaching only to make a living, and that would hinder the gospel. So Paul renounced his right.

Having made application, Paul adds to his argument (v. 13). He uses the example of the "ministers" of the temple. It is doubtful that this could refer to heathen priests and temples, for Paul wished to give no merit to what God had renounced and the Corinthians had turned away from. "Do ye not know" suggests familiar knowledge, and it was well-known that those who worked at sacred things received their livelihood from that. Those who habitually served in the temple received a portion of the altar sacrifice. Part was burned on the altar and part was given to the priests.

Lastly, in this section, Paul notes an argument from the Lord's command (v. 14). This last point is the strongest and highest. Paul has argued naturally, legally, and scripturally. Perhaps he is making a general reference to such passages as Luke 10:7. We cannot be sure. It does tell us, however, that a wide knowledge of the Lord's teaching was a part of both the writer and the readers. And so the point has been made. The Old and the New Testaments have united to make a point. But Paul renounced these rights for the success of the gospel. He shall enlarge on this in the rest of the chapter and prove his example of love in liberty of conscience.

3. The Discipline of Liberty in Conscience (9:15-27)

Paul had not exercised his rights or liberty; the refusal to do so had become the rule. Nor is he writing to establish them for the future. Fiercely, strongly, and with much emotion he announces that "it were better for me to die"; in the Greek, Paul leaves this incompleted. Rather he will hold to his claim. He will never be so dependent. Paul does not boast in the wrong sense. He refers to the progress of the gospel, not to his own accomplishments (v. 15).

Even in the preaching of the gospel, Paul does not "glory" (v. 16). He can claim no real credit there. Rather "necessity" is laid heavily on him. The Greeks considered it ruin to fight against "necessity." Paul thinks of some undefined disaster as coming upon him if he did not preach the gospel. God leaves man the freedom to resist such a divine charge, but the result is judgment. Paul was a man of duty, captured by mercy and grace, once an enemy, not a determined ambassador of the Cross.

Verse 17 may be understood in more than one way. It may be the man who preaches willingly merits a reward; whereas, if unwilling, he is nevertheless not excused. Or perhaps to be preferred is the idea that this verse is built on the previous one. If he preached from choice he would merit a reward. As it is, it is not his own choice; he must preach. The following verse would then begin, "What reward is possible under these circumstances?" Whatever the choice, the picture is one of a servant whose work is determined for him and his merit is in his faithfulness. The picture is of a sovereign Lord and an obedient slave. Duty was entrusted of the Lord to Paul. But this hint of predestination is in apostleship, not in salvation.

Therefore, Paul's real reward is that while he had to preach, he did not have to preach without pay (v. 18). But from his Master's example, Paul too had learned to be gracious and giving, in a lesser sense. Thus Paul rejects reward in the mercenary sense, to claim it in the wider ethical sense. Again the purpose was not to "abuse" or make full use of his power or right in the gospel, but so the gospel might be more powerfully and successfully spread. Liberty bows to love.

The foundation for this action is stressed; the gospel must be advanced (v. 19). Paul's real aim in this chapter comes into view. It is of liberty asserted and established for the purpose of self-abnegation. Paul did not become unnecessarily encumbered by the demands of men. Rather, he freed himself from everyone so he might truly be everyone's servant. Paul had been faced with the charge of "gainseeking"[106]; gain he did seek—the gaining of many for Christ. And by this course of action he gained many more than otherwise, including those who are listed below.

He "became" to the Jews as a Jew. He had been ostracized by them. But he would not unnecessarily antagonize his own nation (v. 20). An example of this is the circumcision of Timothy in Acts 16:3. Paul did not believe the law of Moses could save a man nor did he agree with the binding Jewish ceremonies and traditions. He was under grace not law.[107] But he respected Jewish scruple and conformed to practices that would enable him to more acceptably approach the Jews. There is no hint of "watering down" his beliefs. Rather this is a subjection of accommodation not of principle. He would not be bound to obey the Law, but he did so voluntarily. "Them that are under the law" would include those above and also circumcised proselytes. This brought on Paul the reproach of "still preaching circumcision." But this misinterprets this passage. Always the goal is there: ". . . that I might gain them. . . ."

Paul mentions the Gentiles, or those "without law" (v. 21). "Without law" was the Jewish designation for all outside the cover of Mosaism. This Paul abandoned in that he did not practice the law of Moses among the Gentiles or make it the basis for his preaching. But Paul was not "without law" in the wider, true, Christian sense. Paul instead had advanced to an even stronger position. He was more than under the Law; he was a slave to Christ. He obeyed the "law of Christ," which is certain of fulfillment because this law is by the Spirit, not as an external yoke, but as "an implanted life." All of this "that I might gain them. . . ."

Third, Paul lists the weak (v. 22). In so doing, he comes to the situation of his readers and also returns us to 1 Corinthians 8. He left his strength and felt their weakness, "that [he] might gain the weak. . . ." The last half of this verse sums up Paul's actions in the various areas of his ministry. Note the thrice-repeated "all." In all these actions no compromise or compliance with unchristian principles is indicated, but rather love and self-denial. Paul did not bend before opposition. But where no principle was at stake, he would go to extreme lengths to meet people and win them to Christ. This Paul expected to be self-evident. "Some" indicates that not all would accept Paul's message, but that did not deter him from attempting to reach as many as possible; in fact, "all" men.

In "all things" (v. 23) Paul's governing aim is the gospel's sake. His one purpose is to fulfill his stewardship of the gospel.[108] Paul is determined and versatile in this complicated situation to achieve his primary goal. His personal ambition is that he might be a joint-partaker in winning salvation with those he leads to Christ and spiritual maturity. This prepares the stage for the following remarks on discipline and speaks to the Corinthians of the fact that if they follow in the right way they too will receive this most excellent of rewards.

The thing suggested is now openly expressed (v. 24). Self-discipline was necessary for both Paul's mission and his salvation. His example was intended to teach his readers their need for this on a personal and church level. Paul relays his message under the illustration of the Isthmian games (which gained their name from the isthmus on which Corinth stood). They were the scene every second (or third) year of huge crowds and great festivities. Only free men could participate in the games and they had to give satisfactory proof that for 10 months before the contest they had participated in the necessary preliminary training. For 30 days before the contest the contestants had to attend exercises at the gymnasium and only after all conditions were fulfilled could they publicly participate in the exercises. The herald announced the name and country of each contestant, and also the name of the winner, who was crowned with a garland of pine needles, parsley, or ivy. The winner's family was honored and when he returned to

81

his native city, a breach was made in the walls to allow him to enter; the purpose being to indicate that the town with such a citizen had no need of walls for its defense. He was immortalized in verse and given a prominent seat at all future contests.[109]

Paul contrasts this with the Christian race. In the Greek games only one won the prize. In the Christian race the prize is open to all. The emphasis is on the disciplined, purposeful, hard-running winner. The Christian should run like the winner runs. The discipline will result in the delight of the reward; the cross in the crown (v. 25). The point is to not mere abstinence but to strong control of appetite and passion. The crown won at the games was the most coveted honor in the Greek world. If some would strive and discipline themselves that much for a "corruptible" wreath, how much harder should we be willing to strive for our "incorruptible" wreath! Observe that the athlete denies himself many lawful pleasures and, in fact, anything that hinders his total effectiveness. The emphasis is on "all things."

The subjection of the body in this manner is illustrated (v. 26) first by the race and the runner; this leads to the illustration of the boxer. Paul will exert his own example to edify the church. He does not run or fight without purpose or aim. He knows where the finish line is. Nor is he shadowboxing; his opponent is real and he lands blows on him. Every ounce of energy is put into purposeful, directed Christian endeavor. It is only by such strenuous effort that Paul will win.

Paul does not maul or bruise his body, but lays it flat with the right blow in the right place (v. 27). He does this so he might meet the test and qualify for his reward. And the victory is a permanent one, for Paul brings his body into subjection and makes it a slave. It appears Paul accepted his severe bodily suffering as needful for his own sanctification. (Also read 1 Peter 4:1ff; Romans 8:13; and Colossians 3:5.) He dared not lose his crown through failure to satisfy his Lord or through carelessness and lack of discipline. The practices of Middle Ages flagellants have been supported by this text, but Paul's discipline was not arbitrary and self-inflicted for personal gain, but dictated by his calling. With this thought on self-discipline then we are smoothly carried into the following section.

82

B. The Limitation in Liberty (10:1 to 11:1)

1. Examples Warning Against Self-indulgence (10:1-13)

Paul has spoken against indulgence and undisciplined liberty on the basis of its danger to others (chapter 8) and its danger to one's effectiveness in service (chapter 9). Now he will address himself to its inherent dangers to the person himself. Indulgence may imperil one's own soul. He begins by turning to Old Testament history. In so doing, he will rebuke the Corinthians' complacency in these matters of conscience and question.

"I would not . . . should be ignorant" (v. 1) indicates the importance of what Paul is saying and its vital nature to the Corinthians as a warning. Paul stresses "*all* our fathers." "All" is repeated five times in the first four verses. Without exception, the Israelites received of the blessings of God. This gives more emphasis to verse 5. The events referred to seem most directly related to the time of the Exodus. "Our fathers" is intended to identify the New Testament church with the Old Testament church. The fate of the fathers teaches and warns the children. These knew the cloud of divine guidance[110] and "passed through the sea," probably the Red Sea.[111] Both the cloud and the sea were glorious signs of God's presence, blessing, strength, and salvation.

Together these experiences constituted the inauguration of Israel's national covenant life. Israel was here born into its divine estate (v. 2). The Israelites were "baptized" unto Moses since in these acts they committed themselves to the leadership of Moses, and "through" him entered acknowledged fellowship with God. There is some admitted emphasis here on the symbolic separation in baptism, and then unification. The Corinthians had also been symbolically "baptized unto Christ." Galatians 3:27 speaks of baptism into Christ, perhaps by the Spirit.[112] The Israelites were united to Moses but this relationship was nowhere as close as the union between Christ and the Christian.

The Israelites were sustained by manna from heaven[113] and water from the rocks of Rephidim and Kadesh (vv. 3, 4).[114] These carried a spiritual meaning for the believing, intelligent partakers. The last half of verse 4 explains the first half. Paul calls the water "spiritual." He doesn't say the rock from which it issued was spiritual and not material, but that there was a "spiritual rock"

83

following them; their spirits drank while their bodies drank. That other rock was the Christ. Paul is thus calling attention to the food's supernatural origin.

Some suppose Paul is adopting the rabbinical legend that the water-bearing Rephidim rock journeyed on with the Israelites. But grammar discards this. Paul would not say the preincarnate Christ followed Israel in the form of a lump of rock. It is the Christ and His person that is referred to here; indicating that He existed in Old Testament times and was spiritually present with Old Testament Israel. It is necessary that the divine Head be so identified to relate the Old Testament example to the New Testament Church. The outcome is then, Christ existed amid this ancient people and yet they perished. How can Christians believe themselves totally secure from the same fate? In passing, the apostle suggests the Lord's Supper is "spiritual food" and "drink" by the first analogy to baptism in 10:2-4 and by the reference to the Eucharist in 10:16-22. Nowhere else in the New Testament are the two so colocated.

Instead of recognizing Christ's presence and blessings, Israel murmured and was disobedient. The contrasting "but" (v. 5) is strong. Therefore, God was displeased and Israel was judged in the wilderness. The greater part died in the wilderness; only Caleb and Joshua reached the Promised Land.[115] "Many" of the "all," so highly favored and blessed, received only God's dire judgment. Why? Because of wrong attitudes which resulted in disobedience. What a point to the Corinthians!

These were to serve as examples and warnings to the Corinthians and to us to avoid similar disobedience for the sake of our own salvation. At the very heart of these disobedient actions were disobedient attitudes, which Paul proceeds to enumerate. The first (v. 6) refers to attitude and desire: "We should not lust." It recalls Numbers 11:4, and the Israelite desire for the old diet of Egypt and at the same time the attraction of the idol-feasts in Corinth. Evil passions desire evil things.

From the general admonition, Paul enlarges his discussion to cover certain particulars (v. 7). He admonishes against idolatry. This urgent warning is repeated in verse 14. Paul draws from Exodus 32:18-20 and quotes 32:6. Here was the danger for the Corinthians. They had been delivered from the superstition of heathen religion, but they were still drawn by its festivities. Enjoying this wild, careless merriment could lead rather easily to idolatry. Also note that the Israelites did this at a time when they were waiting to receive the divine Law from God by Moses.

From lust and desire to idolatry to fornication the progression moves (v. 8). Paul's primary reference appears to be Numbers 25. Paul records that 23,000 died, while Numbers 25:9 records that 24,000 died. Paul may be allowing for those killed by the judges in Numbers 25:5; an error could have been committed by an early copier of the text; or, perhaps best, round numbers are used. Such a difference does not take away from the serious danger possible in this situation.

The natural progression is simply stated by Paul (v. 9). The next step is tempting Christ. First has come sensuality; now comes unbelief. The Corinthians would commit this same sin of presuming on divine forbearance if they continued to trifle with idolatry and these related sins. It is extremely foolish to try God to see how far He will let us go in sin before He brings judgment to bear. Israel tempted God; the result was judgment from God in the form of fiery serpents. At Corinth it was not so much the participation in pagan feasts as it was dissatisfaction with the restrictions on their new faith that caused the problem.[116]

A fifth item is added: murmuring. This amounts to disbelief of God's goodness and is the total opposite of faith in God. Paul may be referring to the rebellion of Korah in Numbers 16:41. Such murmuring was visited by the destroyer or "death angel."[117] Such defiance always meets its doom before Almighty God.

Having drawn his illustrations from Old Testament history, Paul then proceeds to apply them and the lessons taught to the present (v. 11). "Now" indicates summarization and application. These admonitions are for those "upon whom the ends of the world are come." Jewish and pagan history and their ends are alike disclosed in Christianity; the two converge at this central point. The final era is the Christian era and all history converges on and finds its apex in this era. For the lessons of history to go unheeded by this generation would be disastrous.

Paul wants his readers to be spiritually wary and alert to the dangers of sin. "Standeth" (v. 12) refers to our position in Christ. The problem is basically that of pride. The Corinthians had the same proud attitudes of those ancient Israelites; and unless corrected, the results could be the same. They would "fall," sin, morally fall. For this reason, Paul writes a strong warning to watchfulness: "Take heed" that you do stand.

But the example that alarms the proud may give hope to the burdened and discouraged; this trial and temptation is bearable. Paul offers consolation (v. 13) first in the fact that this temptation is common to man; it is such as can be borne; it is measured by the strength of the tempted. Further consolation is found in the fact that God does not originate the temptation, but He does control it. God is faithful to help. Consolation is furthered by the fact that God not only limits it, He also supplies the escape. The purpose of seeing the escape is that the tempted may be able to bear the trial. He can hold up under it. The Corinthians faced the temptation of idolatry and its counterparts and, if resisted, the possibility of persecution. But the door stood open in Christ to help. The temptation would not merely leave; it could be conquered!

2. *Abstinence From Idolatry (10:14-22)*

Having added general admonitions, Paul now zeros in on a particular problem and by so doing adds another principle to this section on questions of conscience. "Indulgence may identify with the world" and we must not provoke Christ to jealousy.

Verse 14 could certainly apply to what has just been said; it seems also to fit well, and perhaps best, with what follows, simply because 10:15-22 makes a more specific application to idolatry and its accompanying dangers. Ultimately this verse serves as a hinge for the chapter. "My dearly beloved" expresses great concern and deep emotion on the part of the apostle. As he had counseled regarding fornication in 6:18, he does here regarding idolatry. "Flee" is the admonition. The Corinthians were not to casually view sin and linger in it; they were to fly from its presence. They were not to see how far they could go, but to have nothing to do with sin. Paul had promised them God's sustenance in time of temptation, but this was not a license to play with sin; rather, flee it!

The Corinthians prided themselves on their wisdom. Whether Paul mixes sarcasm into his statement (v. 15) or not, he writes in such a way as to appeal to their attitude and thereby achieve his point. If they are really sensible, they will judge and see the wisdom of what Paul writes. But it must be their decision.

Paul hopes that as they judge they will come to understand the matter of fellowship and communion in this discussion. Communion (v. 16) will be of utmost importance as Paul discusses communion with Christ and communion with demons and how the two are incompatible. Two elements are involved in such fellowship: one has to do with the sacred object or person honored; the other has to do with the common association among the celebrants. The cup was blessed and hallowed by Christ; thus Paul's reference to the "cup of blessing." "Cup of blessing" was the name given to the third cup of the Passover meal and may have been the cup with which our Lord instituted the ordinance of Holy Communion. It seems both natural and within the realm of the Corinthians' experience for Paul to refer to it at this point. Morris affirms that "bless" refers to the kind of prayer that was used over the cup, although that prayer's purpose was to consecrate the cup to a holy use. The reference would then be to the prayer of thanksgiving said over the cup.[118]

Paul has a much wider view, however, than just "blessing" the cup and "breaking" the bread. He has in view the whole sacred affair by which we have communion with Christ. The emphasis here is on the breaking by which "one" was given to "many" and they in turn again become one! These elements are a "communion" of the blood and body of Christ, which takes us to the life, death, and resurrection of Jesus Christ. A covenant was formed. Our communion then is based on a covenant formed because of the Cross. Therefore, the emphasis is on fellowship in Christ. It is difficult to assert doctrines like transubstantiation or consubstantiation on the basis of this verse. The fact of participation is asserted; the nature of such participation must be built from other sources.

The presiding theme is unity (v. 17). A single loaf was used at Communion, which symbolized unity. The place of Communion in bringing about unity is indicated by the phrase beginning "for." The ordinance stems from unity and creates unity for those who partake. They are one in spirit, one in faith, and one in worship.

The difficulty in this verse rests with the phrase, "For . . .

body." This is often construed as a continued dependent clause. We could then translate: "Since we who are many are one bread, one body"; or, "Since there (is) one bread (and), we, the many, are one body." However, the first translation confuses the figures and identifies the "bread" with the Church itself. The second artificially supplies "and" and reverses bread and body; improperly making the body the ground.[119] The better translation seems to be: "Seeing that there is one bread, we the many, are one body." One last note must be added. The "bread" suggests the idea of a common nourishment, sustaining and strengthening an identical life.

To enlarge his discussion, Paul turns to the observances of "Israel after the flesh" (v. 18) for illustration. This expression distinguishes the nation of Israel from the Church, the true Israel. Paul points to the fact that those who "eat of the sacrifices" are "partakers" or have communion with the altar. Further participation in the sacrificial feast means fellowship in the sacrifice. Paul's mind is on the total Israelite communion.[120] There was a recognition of fellowship and service. Needless to say it was no small thing to eat of the sacrifices offered on the burnt altar in the Jewish temple.

Paul is pointing to a climax (vv. 19, 20). He has brought out the meaning of the Lord's Supper and the communion involved to prove the danger of attending idol-feasts. Certain of the men of "knowledge" at Corinth would argue that idolatry is merely illusion; there is no genuine ground of reality especially for the Christian.[121] The idol-feasts have no religious meaning and do not touch their consciences; therefore, friendship or social involvement should allow them to go. Paul admits the truth of the nonreality of the idol in itself in 8:4. But he realizes the terrible presences behind the idol. Demons are worshiped and communicated with at these heathen feasts. The riot and perversion attending these festivals showed evil spirits presided over the events and Satan prompted the idolatry.[122] Therefore, the sacrifice is really being offered to evil spirits and fellowship is established by the sharing of food.[123]

The position of those Corinthian Christians who ate the Lord's Supper and still conformed to participation in idol-feasts was untenable (vv. 21, 22). Paul is not properly speaking of the physical impossibility, but of the moral and spiritual impossibility of true participation in both the Lord's communion and the devil's communion. As there cannot be two masters, so there cannot be two communions. The distinct reference to both the "cup" and the "table" emphasizes the strong nature of this admonition. "Cup of the Lord" and like phrases indicate possession and leadership. The Lord distributes it and it denotes allegiance and true fellowship with Him. Therefore, participation in idol-feasts is dangerous and really impossible because of the fellowship with demons which it allows and even establishes. This is the true situation; to oppose it is to break fellowship with the Lord and thus provoke Him to jealousy. The allusion is to Deuteronomy 32:21. To do this is to suppose that we, including Paul, are stronger than He is. Such an idea is obviously foolish.

3. Unselfish Profit in Privilege (10:23 to 11:1)

Rather, there must be expedient and edifying profit in our actions (v. 23). "All things are lawful" states the great, general principle of liberty. It is repeated twice. It may have been a popular cry with the Corinthians. Paul even repeats part of the statement in 6:12. But not everything is in our best interest, or another's. Expedient refers to what is wise, beneficial, and most proper at the moment. Edify refers to building up, especially in the Christian faith. The point is not whether or not it is allowable, but whether or not it is profitable in a Christian manner. The pervading theme in Paul's conclusion on the eating of sacrificial meats, the questions of conscience, is the supremacy of love in church life, expressed by edification. Love is superior to knowledge (8:1) and is the guard of liberty (10:23-33). It should be noted that when Paul speaks of edifying he has more than just the weak in mind. The whole Church, the Christian community, must be safeguarded by love, and thus edified. Paul further narrows down this principle in verse 24. The Christian is to seek the good of others and promote their interests, not his own. The American Standard Version uses the phrase "his neighbor's good."

Therefore, on the basis of these principles, Paul explains what should be done about idol-meat offered in the meat market for sale (vv. 25, 26). Idol-meat was often difficult to avoid because the butcher generally burnt at least a few hairs of an animal as a sacrifice and the priest would often sell extra meat in the market.[124] Paul says to ask no question about it; rather, accept the fact that it is a blessing of the Lord, "for the earth is the Lord's."[125] It would have been difficult to discover the nature of the meat being sold in such a shop. To have done so would probably have caused trouble. In such a situation the Christian should recognize the divine origin and goodness of the Lord and rest in that. "This means that the Christians, who rule with Christ over all things (3:23), may freely use them (Romans 14:14, 20). But they must use them according to the law of God."[126]

A second specific situation is listed with advice (v. 27). This involves being invited to a dinner by an unsaved host. When one goes, whatever is set before him should be eaten without questioning the origin of the food. This involves a private meal not a meal in an idol temple. Before an unbelieving host or family, the Christian will be narrowly watched. One of the great dangers here is offense or unprofitable action. In such a situation, the Christian should not ask foolish questions on scruples that have no merit. He should eat what is set on the table. There is no need to raise the question of conscience in the one situation any more than in the other.

But at some time at such a dinner or in a marketplace, someone may approach the Christian and explain that the meat has been sacrificed first to an idol. Paul states specifically what should be done. The situation has been altered. The speaker is evidently troubled by such knowledge and the strong Christian should refrain from eating. The meat is now not simply a gift of God, having passed through unknown sources. Rather, it is known as the end-product of idolatry and some believed that to then eat would mean idolatry. The Christian must not eat "for conscience' sake."[127] But Paul does not mean the conscience of the eater, but the conscience of the speaker. The eater is apparently a stronger Christian who realizes that offering meat to an idol cannot really alter its nature or character. The speaker, or another, cannot see or grab this. Therefore, in deference to this weaker conscience, the strong Christian should not eat such meat. In summation, whether the speaker is a weak Christian or a pagan, and whether the intent is to warn or embarrass, at such a point the Christian should announce his faith, and for the sake of another abstain from eating "sacrifice-meat."

Two interconnected questions are further set forth in the discussion (vv. 29, 30). Why should anyone else be able to guide and limit my actions? As long as I eat with a heart of thankfulness to God, why should I be discredited for doing so? The underlying motive for Paul's words is that the exercise of liberty must not be made the means of offense to another. Certainly the Christian here eats with a spirit of thanksgiving. And Paul does not wish that an action in this worthy spirit should cause evil speaking among those who do not see it in the same light. By the first question Paul really states that nothing would be gained by the exercise of liberty here. He says of liberty what he says of faith in Romans 14:22. With the second question the strong implication is that definite harm could result. Thanksgiving here leads to blasphemy. A person with a sensitive conscience seeing the Christian offer thanks knowingly over idol-meat would regard the ·act as sacrilegious indulgence and hypocrisy.

There must, therefore, be that necessary consideration of others in what we do. While there is a limit to which another conscience or person should be regarded, nevertheless, consideration for others must be added to our liberty, our free personal conscience, and our true thanksgiving to God for His gifts.

As he concludes, Paul gives two major reasons for acting as he has admonished (v. 31). The first is that all may redound to the glory of God. All thoughts of personal liberty, assertion of rights, all actions, eating, drinking—anything and everything—must be subordinate to the supreme maxim of Christian duty; bringing glory to God. This must be so in the ordinary things of life. The statement is simple yet all-inclusive, general yet deep and demanding. May "all" bring glory to God.

The second reason is that there be no occasion to stumble for anyone, in or outside the Church (v. 32). "Jews" and "Gentiles" include all outside the Church. Christian believers alone form "the church of God." This Church is bound tightly to the glory of God and must refrain from self-indulgence. Causing another to stumble would result in the other sinning. And that would, of course, affect his salvation and bring dishonor to the Lord. Paul wants his readers to be fully aware of their need for love and concern at this point. We must be careful. This is not to say that some may wrongly take offense, but we are not to give offense. We must draw men closer to Jesus Christ.

Paul concludes by using himself as an example of what he means (10:33; 11:1). The apostle attempts to teach not only from knowledge but also from personal life and example. No personal advantage is intended; he seeks the salvation of many and thus does not do what is pleasing to himself. And in this Paul urges his readers to imitate him. Yet even as he does this, he points them away from himself. He urges that they imitate him only because and as he imitates Christ. Paul does not seek his own profit. Yet when it seems he is giving up spiritual and material gain for others, suddenly he has gained eternal life and great spiritual wealth. "The many" are contrasted with the single self.

Paul did everything he could for the salvation of many. And in losing he gained; in giving he received; in surrendering he won. His aim was the highest; his goal the best. This is the proper balance of liberty and love.

VI

Public
Worship
(11:2 to 14:40)

A. Sanctity and Honor in Worship (11:2-16)

This is a new section in Paul's letter to the Corinthians. It deals primarily with abuses in what we would call public worship. He discusses women wearing a covering in public and while praying or prophesying. He discusses the gifts of the Spirit and the body of Christ; the great discourse on love is in this chapter, and then he returns to a specific discussion of tongues (and interpretation) and prophecy. He will answer some very difficult questions in the verses that follow.

The immediate paragraph deals with sanctity in worship by all, but particularly Paul speaks regarding women. Some have denounced Paul as a woman hater because of what he writes here and in chapter 7. Yet it was Paul who insisted that all distinctions between Jew and Greek, bond and free, male and female are removed in the Lord. All will certainly agree that much of what Paul writes here concerns a local and temporary custom of dress. Today we would not insist women actually wear veils when attending worship services. But there is a principle here that must be closely observed. It is this: The mental, moral, and spiritual equality of the sexes is consistent with the dependence, submission, and obedience of a wife to her husband.

Unfortunately, the teaching of equality had been misunderstood at Corinth and so this latter principle of submission was being cast aside. Paul insists on maintaining the custom of veils principally because of the reasons it had been discarded. He asserts the principle of subordination, which is necessary for maintenance of sanctity and honor in (public) worship.

Paul wishes always to hear and believe the best possible regarding the Corinthians, so he opens with a note of commendation and praise (v. 2). They are praised for remembering Paul and holding "fast" what he has taught them. But it is necessary for Paul to qualify this commendation. He delights in praising wherever he can; here, unfortunately, it must be tempered with instruction. In verse 4 Paul will begin with a subject the Corinthians failed completely to understand in principle.

For even here it appears Paul is delivering some new lesson (v. 3). Paul intends to show the Corinthians why the veiling of women is the best thing to do. He wants his readers to do it intelligently and for the right reasons. Therefore, he explains the principle of subordination and the order of authority. "Head" refers to a governing, controlling, ruling organ. It indicates a relationship of superior authority. The authority is not defined precisely, but then none of the relationships in this verse are precisely the same. "The head of every man is Christ" begins the discussion of authority. The Head equals the Christ.[128] Each man has one head, Christ. Paul thus states the violated principle. The title "the Christ" includes the wide scope of His offices and conveys His very definite position as God and Head, the seat of authority. He is every man's true head for He is the "one Lord" of all creation.

"The head of the woman is the man," establishes the order of authority God has ordained. Man holds headship directly from His Creator and is brought by his manhood into direct responsibility to Christ. This would appear to be wider than just the Christian realm. Faith is common to man and woman. The parallel assertions must rest on a common basis. The very law of marriage and the social order are grounded in Christ. "Head" lacks the article and "woman" lacks "every," which deems this less absolute than Christ over man. But nevertheless, in the Church as well as in nature the man is over the woman.

In the directly related side of submission, again the Lord of nature set the pattern with His perfect loyalty and obedience to the Father. This should make it easier for the woman, to see that Christ is subject to God the Father and man to the Head, Christ. In nature there is equality; in office and work there is submission.

This principle applied directly to the veiling of women. Paul first writes of the unveiled man (v. 4). This was strictly Christian, for the Jewish male covered his head. Also the action is of praying or prophesying. This involves other people and therefore must be public in scope. This custom was not limited to these actions but these probably called notable attention to the apparel. "Having his head covered" involves the principle of subordination. Man's only head is Christ, and while both sexes worship Him in common, woman also has man as her head. He must not wear a veil or he acts like a woman, and she must or she acts like a man. The man who wears a covering dishonors his "head," or his own place, and acts as though he had a human head over him. This reflects on Christ, for he shames Christ whose lordship he represents.

The identical situation is repeated for the woman (v. 5). But it is necessary for the woman to have her head covered as a sign of submission to the man. If she does not do so she dishonors her "head." The dishonor done to the dominant sex falls on her and the shame comes home to her, as is shown in verse 5. It is also a reflection on Christ's lordship and order of authority.

Among the Greeks only prostitutes went about unveiled; slavewomen wore the shaven head, as did the punished adulteress.[129] By unveiling herself, the Christian woman identified herself with these and abandoned the principle of subordination.[130] With force Paul asserts the principle and pattern.

The point is enlarged (v. 6). The reasoning is analogous. It would be agreed that it was a shame for a woman to be shaved or shorn. It is unwomanly, rather manly. So is not wearing a veil. Therefore, the woman who begins to act like a man by unveiling should be consistent and be shorn also. But having the head shorn or shaved is a shame, as can be clearly seen and admitted. Therefore, having the head unveiled is also a shame; thus, the veil should be used. By this analogy the woman can see the end result of her action and resume her rightful place as a woman honorable and veiled.

Paul draws an argument for his position from the story of creation (v. 7).[131] Man was made in the direct image and glory of God. Woman appears, in creation, as derived and auxiliary. It is as wrong for the man to cover his head as it is for the woman not to. For man to veil himself would be to hide the "image and glory of God." Paul adds to image, glory. Paul understands the Genesis account to refer especially to the male, although no particular sex distinction is there noted. Man is the pinnacle of creation and shows forth God's glory. Therefore, there should be no sign of subordination when a man worships. Woman, in her right, stands in a position, singular in nature, to the man and therefore is "the glory of the man." This affords her a high position and at the same time protects man's position. She is the glory, not of the race, but of the stronger sex. At the same time she is his counterpart. Faith, purity, and beauty show most excellently and proportionately in her. The man who degrades a woman degrades his manhood and shows the measure of his human dignity.

Further explanation for verse 7 follows in verses 8 and 9. Two more are added to the chain of "fors" beginning at verse 6. Paul has origin (v. 8) and purpose (v. 9) in creation in mind. There is a reference to Genesis 2:21-24. In origin woman came from Adam's rib and in purpose she was to be his helper and companion. Originally in creation man did not come from woman, nor was he created for her. He came first. These facts stand forever. To ignore, discredit, or disallow this arrangement of God is to invite problems and resultant loss and harm.

Verse 10 offers some difficulties in the discussion however. Phrases such as "power on her head"[132] and "because of the angels," must be explained. An important factor is the context. Paul has been speaking of the principle of subordination, and particularly of the design and purpose of woman in creation. The first phrase would seem to refer to that to which she submits, the veil being its symbol. The soldier under the queen's colors might be said "to have authority over his head."[133] Shakespeare wrote, "Present him eminence both with eye and tongue" (Macb. iii, 4), and used it to express the authority of another pictured in oneself.

"Because of the angels" has received various interpretations over the centuries, some improbable, some impossible. Paul cannot mean evil angels subject to sensual temptation. Some have seen in these angels: pious men, prophets, church officers, and matchmakers. Some have suggested changes in the text, and some would delete the words as a gloss.[134] But the better interpretation seems to be as follows. In 1 Corinthians 4:9, Paul mentioned the angels as interested observers of Christian conduct. In 6:3, he spoke of the judgment of certain angels by the saints.

Scripture is filled with the fact that angels are associated with God's earthly kingdom.[135] They are connected with the maintenance of creational laws and limits. It is, therefore, consistent that the angels are present at divine worship and are disturbed and offended by irreverence and poor conduct at such worship.[136] J. A. Fitzmyer notes passages in the Dead Sea Scrolls in which men with a blemish (such as crippled or diseased, etc.) were excluded from the army or the assembly, because of the presence of angels. No unseemliness should come before them.[137]

But Paul also wants to insure the proper position of both man and woman, their need for each other, and their equality under God. There is a basic equality and responsibility of both to each other and God. The woman is subordinate but not inferior (v. 11). Christianity recognizes the rights of women as nowhere in heathenism; and in the higher things, "in the Lord" and in faith, man and woman exist in partnership and equality.

There is a balance between equality and subordination (v. 12). Man is the initial cause; woman the instrumental cause. But the direct, original Source and Ruler over all is the one Father—God—to whom both owe a single reverence. This makes man only a relative source.

Paul asks his readers to look at this carefully and judge; the inference being that they will come up with the same reasoning he has presented (v. 13). "Yourselves" is emphatic. They can discover the truth for themselves. There is an appeal to the fitness and suitability of things to nature or character. There is an appeal to the readers' common sense. There is an appeal to the fact that it was commonly agreed a woman should be veiled. The question hinges on general propriety and the Christian influence involved with it, and Paul is sure when the Corinthians rightly consider this custom they will not find it improper.

Paul appeals to the instincts and teaching of nature to support a related item; that of a man's short hair and a woman's long hair (vv. 14, 15). He refers to man's moral constitution. The idea of a man wearing short hair has prevailed in modern times as it did in ancient times. There have, however, been exceptions. Homer's warriors wore long hair and the fashion was retained at Sparta. But the Athenian cropped his head when 18 and it was a mark of effeminacy, except for the aristocratic knights, to let the hair grow long. The Nazirite was another exception. Yet even today, for the majority, this custom prevails.

On the other hand, a woman's long hair is her glory. It is the crown of her beauty. Her hair has been given to her to serve as a covering or hood, not to do away with the veil but to match it as a covering. Thus, her glory is founded upon her humility. We must remember Paul's reasons for his remarks here. It is necessary that there be a clear distinction of the sexes in appearance as well as every other natural and scriptural way. And there also remains this principle of subordination; the man to Christ and the woman to man.

Abruptly Paul cuts off the discussion with the words on custom and contention in verse 16. Contentious refers to a quarrelsome person, one who disputes for the sake of disputation. It seems this attitude among the Corinthians touched everything, a woman's veil or the position of an arch-apostle. The condition of reality suggests Paul also expected some to be contentious in this matter.

The problem with this verse lies in the interpretation and reference of "we have no such custom." Some have argued that this refers to "being contentious." Paul and his fellow workers and, in fact, all the assemblies of God in unanimity were seeking not strife, but peace, order, and proper actions. Their ultimate intent would be not to burden any with what was not necessary to salvation or to judge that others had sinned when they broke one of these customs without offense to others. Many who support this view link this verse with verse 17.

Some, however, argue that "custom" refers to what is described in verse 4 and following. A contentious temper would never be indulged by Paul. Those who supported unveiling of women may have supposed that Paul, the champion of liberty, supported them and that the veil was being rejected elsewhere also. Paul here denies both suppositions.

Many deviations have appeared based on one of these two major interpretations. The time has not been taken to list them. The latter view appears stronger on the basis of context and principle. Paul is then saying, "We have no such custom such as women praying or prophesying with head uncovered."[138] Paul appeals to universal custom and to the fact that this is the habit throughout the Christian churches. Otherwise, if the former view is adopted, it would seem Paul is doing away somewhat with what he has just spent 15 verses asserting. That is not like Paul.

Paul intended that the Corinthians do what was proper, best, and seemly in their situation. That involved obeying the custom of veiled women and unveiled men. But Paul was not defending a custom per se. He was supporting the principle with which the custom was linked and which it represented—subordination. In the Western world of our day, the custom of a veil or covering is not generally followed, but the principle remains unchanged. There must be a clear distinction of the sexes, the clear assertion of roles, and the proper order of authority that God established.

B. The Observance of the Lord's Supper (11:17-34)

Paul turns to another important matter, the Lord's Supper. Rather than the expected praise, Paul strongly censures the Corinthians for their actions at this ordinance. Divisions and gross self-centeredness were damaging the sacredness of church fellowship and worship. Paul needed to set these problems in order.

In the previous section, Paul corrected an error that may have been the result of ignorance. Not so this problem. This was a glaring fault that had to be corrected and Paul does so with authority (v. 17). The content of and reason for the censure is set forth. The Corinthians came together "for the worse" instead of the better. Their church meetings were profitless. This Lord's Supper, which should have been hallowed and unifying, was the climax of profitlessness, desecration, and disgrace.

Paul specifies the causes of this disgraceful gathering (v. 18). "For first of all" introduces the first reason. The second may be found in verse 34 or the whole of chapters 12 through 14. The main idea that Paul wishes to pursue is involved. "When ye come together" indicates repeated, continuous occurrence. The trouble was chronic. When they gathered together they "always" brought their contentious spirit with them. The problem listed here is disunity and lack of harmony. Chapter 1 comes into focus again, this time in the public assembly. Paul had heard various reports on his readers' actions. He does not believe everything he has heard, but he does accept as truth what he lists here. We do

99

not know why he expresses himself precisely as he does. Perhaps he distrusted part of the message. But the proper Christian attitude is present of believing, hoping always the best possible, according to 13:7.

There were factions in the Corinthian church and Paul shows a reason for them (v. 19). There are contending views on this verse: (1) These divisions are inevitable and a purpose of God is served for they sift the loyal from the disloyal, the good from the bad. There are grammatical supports for this view.[139] At this point the designation is parties within the church. The factions leave the genuine believers standing out (approved) by their loyalty, strength, and constancy. Those approved with God become manifest to other men. But there is a necessary test before manifested approval.

A suggested refinement is that (2) Paul is referring to action expressing itself in discussion but not separation. Such discussion would show which Christians were best founded in their faith, but not create divisions.[140] (3) Another view is that the Corinthians felt they had to have factions among them, so those who so highly valued human wisdom could feel superior to everyone else.[141] The first view seems most favorable. But it must be remembered Paul is not advocating factions or divisions. He is simply stating that in this sinful world such will happen. Necessity rather than propriety is the issue here.

The "therefore" of verse 20 expects a conclusion on what has just been said, and at the same time lays a foundation for further remarks. These divisions produced a visible rift at this common meal, making the reality of the Lord's Supper an impossibility. It is impossible to connect what is done among the Corinthians with the true sacrament of the Lord's Supper. The reference is to a larger occurrence than just Holy Communion, as the following verses shall show.

Paul's description reveals scandalous behavior (v. 21). The problem is one of gluttonous, self-centered disregard for anyone else. The "Lord's Supper" as designated here was a united supper with which the meeting of the church commenced, apparently taking place as often as once a week. This church supper, later called the *Agape,* was akin to the dinners held by the guilds and societies so numerous among the Greeks. It originated as a kind of enlarged family meal; it accorded so well with social custom that it was a universal Christian custom in the first century. Later the Communion was separated from the meal for greater decorum and the *Agape* faded into extinction. Each guest brought contributions to supply the table; the poor bringing whatever meager amount they had, the rich bringing out of their abundance. But at the Lord's table He was forgotten. In haste and greed, the Corinthians consumed their own supply as soon as they arrived. The poor man whose supply was insufficient and who might arrive late because his time was not his own found the table empty, the fellowship gone, and he remained hungry. And to add to the ugly picture, hunger and drunkenness sat together. What a terrible thing to happen at, of all places, the Lord's Supper. *Agape* feast indeed! To call it such under these circumstances would have been a travesty.

Paul's pointed questions (v. 22) dramatically and graphically explain the seriousness of the abuses described. Paul's first question proves that home is the place to satisfy such hunger and thirst. His irony slams at the Corinthians' greed and pride. Paul's second question exposes the fact that if this action is deliberate, then they scorn and despise the church—"of God" shows its great place and dignity—and insult the poorer brethren. What coarse contempt is displayed! They ignore everything but their own demands and wants; they publicly shame humbler Christians, and thus do violence to the dignity of the whole church of Jesus Christ. The latter two questions and the last declaration show remarkable restraint by the apostle Paul. He is setting the stage for what is to follow. But he does make it abundantly clear that no praise can be given. This is action for reprimand not praise.

Because Paul wishes to correct such behavior, he holds up before them, as a mirror, the institution, design, and meaning of the Supper as begun by the Lord himself. This is almost certainly the earliest account we have of the institution of Holy Communion. It was written before any of the Gospels and describes in detail this action (some details of which are found nowhere else in Scripture). What Paul passes on (v. 23) came "of the Lord." What Paul received he gave out. He delivered truth correctly, openly, and positively. He, by this, fulfilled his trust.

The phrase "same night . . . betrayed . . ." displays more than a

101

necessary time element for history. It speaks of the character of Jesus who determined to make this new covenant with His people and fulfill the entire will of God even in the dark shadow of betrayal and death. Note also the detail in Paul's teaching. Jesus "took bread" or the unleavened cakes of Passover. But the Corinthians were not following Christ's example and Paul's teaching.

The detail and solemnity of the occasion continue (v. 24). Christ pronounced a blessing of thanks which inaugurated this ordinance, and then turned to the sacraments. Paul's account is similar to that of Luke. There followed first the breaking of the bread, being symbolic of the body of Jesus.[142] What happened to Christ's body was for us.

The words, "This is my body. . . ," have initiated a long controversy between those who favor the idea of a "real" presence of the Lord in the elements and those who favor a "representative" presence of the Lord by the elements. These words have been the primary support for those who support consubstantiation, which supposes the actual body and blood of Christ to exist "in, with, or under" the bread and wine; no permanent association being stated; the relationship being confined to the sacramental action. Transubstantiation supposes the real substance of the bread and wine is changed into that of the body and blood of Christ, while the perceptible characteristics of the elements are not changed.

Without intending a major support for the various arguments, note a few supports for the "representative" or symbolic Communion. Since "this" refers to the "bread" and "for you" is joined to "body," the word *is* cannot imply a complete identity but rather a close connection. The presence of the article before "body" does not justify the conclusion that the head is identified with the body. The article is necessary for purely grammatical reasons. There is a correspondence of relation here rather than of substance. Verse 25 points out that "cup" is connected with "covenant" *(ASV)*. What the Blood effects, the cup sets forth and seals. There is an equal analogy between bread and body. The Communion leads to Christ. It is done in remembrance of Him, which involves confession and consecration, the realization of His great work of atonement, and the sure hope of His return. Faith appropriates the blessings of the ordinance.

"Which is . . . for you" states the purpose of Christ's work. It was done for us, the world. It was done to draw God and man together and bridge the gap of sin. It has a very personal and powerful application. "This do" is present continuous. The design of the institution was that it be continually reenacted until Christ returns. "Of me" is emphatic and again asserts the centrality of Christ in the nature of this act.

Having described Jesus' actions with the bread, Paul describes the place and purpose of the cup (v. 25). The two actions fashion into one covenant. "When he had supped" emphasizes the distinction and special importance of this meal. The impression gathered is that the bread was partaken of during the meal and the cup at the end, although both were necessary parts of Communion. This forged a new "testament" or covenant, initiated by God. In the Old Testament Israel had entered into a "covenant" with God and become His chosen people. But as Jeremiah 31:31-34 prophesied, this old covenant would be replaced by a new covenant founded on forgiveness of sins and the operation of the Holy Spirit within in a new way. The shedding of Christ's blood established the new covenant and all it guaranteed. Christ's death is the basis then for the new covenant which the cup represents. Jesus described no set time for this Communion, but Paul assumed it would be often and that it should be guided by the Lord's instructions on it.

Christ commanded His disciples to perpetually commemorate Him by Communion. But here familiarity had made the service seem common. Paul reminds the Corinthians that they show forth the Lord's death and all it means every time they partake of the sacrament (v. 26). This is really a sermon to men on the activity of God. The rite is to show the Lord's death "till he come." It looks not only back to Calvary, but also ahead to Christ's return and the Marriage Supper of the Lamb. We know not the time or date of this event, but it is an imminent, future fact!

"Wherefore" (v. 27), there are certain conclusions to be drawn on the matter. A judgment of sorts is necessary on those who were violating the table of the Lord. Throughout this passage the verbs speak of continued practice and habit. "Whosoever" excludes no one. Everyone, rich or poor, high or low, needs to approach Communion in a reverent, humble manner. By doing violence to the sacraments, they were actually desecrating the sacrifice and

103

person of the Lord himself. The magnitude of such a sin is measured by the magnitude of the gift. Of equal measure is the just due.

Great care in behavior should be taken toward the Communion. Paul's readers must guard their behavior by making an honest self-examination and then partaking of the elements. Any truly serious attempt at self-probing would make the scene of verses 20-22 impossible. And this must be continually done. Examination would properly involve confession, repentance over anything that blocks the importance of the Lord's Supper and its full significance, and an analysis of one's true faith in Christ. The implication is that the examination will prove fruitful and favorable. Throughout this section, Paul impresses on his readers the tremendous solemnity and importance of this ordinance invoked by the Lord and how terrible is unworthy participation.

Paul emphasizes the great necessity of worthy conduct and self-examination at the Lord's Supper by stressing the judgment that rests on those who do not properly discern the "Lord's body."[143] This verse depicts clearly the carnality of the Corinthians by their approach to Communion. They did not judge or act rightly regarding the elements; therefore, a sentence of judgment rested on them.[144]

Paul bears down on the situation, pointing out that because certain of them did not properly discern "the Lord's body" a sentence of judgment rested on them, with the results that they were weak and sick, and some had even died (v. 30). A literal physical affliction had settled on the Corinthians because they had desecrated the Lord's Supper. However, "sleep" would indicate these had died in Christ, which would appear to justify the view that this visitation had affected more than just the desecrators of the Communion; the church community was suffering for this widespread offense. Paul has in mind, not "natural" effects of excesses, but a special chastening of the Lord. This is additional proof of their disturbing behavior at the Lord's table. It argues that Paul's earlier words were warranted. The readers should correct their attitude and approach and bear the fruits of repentance.

Paul provides the antidote to continued judgment and final condemnation in a two-step sequence (vv. 31, 32); we should judge ourselves. That would solve any problems immediately. But if we do not, the Lord judges and chastens us so we will repent and avoid final condemnation with the "world" of unbelievers. Even in the midst of such sin, Paul exhorts positive advice. The Lord has no desire to see His children fall, so He disciplines them to show them their error and help them return to Him and His way. Paul, in his loving and concerned manner, with his great pastor's heart, uses "we" to associate himself with his readers and the church troubles. Again, a tremendous amount of hope and faith is present. Christ is overshadowing His church and is concerned about each member, and He will keep and accomplish His will and pleasure in the believer.

"Wherefore" (vv. 33, 34) draws us to the second step in Paul's antidote. It is a practical admonition that includes a note of warmth and closeness ("my brethren") after his severe rebuke. The actions of the feast and Lord's Supper must be governed by a loving and reverent spirit. Self-examination will result in mutual accommodation. Therefore, Paul admonishes them to wait for each other. Those who arrive early should wait for those arriving later. Each individual must be of equal importance in the church. No one should begin supper until the whole church has gathered. Waiting for others presumes wanting to feast with them.

Someone might object that he is hungry when he arrives and cannot wait. Paul quiets that objection with the direction to eat something at home first in such cases. The church supper is more for fellowship than bodily fulfillment. To do otherwise is to exclude Christian thought and charity. To do this will avoid the sentence of judgment, the chastisement of the Lord; the spirit of love will once more prevail and the error will be corrected.

Paul adds a footnote to his remarks, "and the rest . . . when I come." Some take this as filling out the "first of all" in verse 18, and see it as referring to different matters that he would pursue. But Paul is probably referring to other features of the administration of the ordinance. The apostle does not set a specific time or occasion for his coming. He is not certain, but under this contingency particular matters must be set in order. With these words Paul concludes his remarks on the Lord's Supper and its proper celebration. It is an invaluable guide for today; for our place in and our approach to Communion.

C. The Cornerstone of True Spirituals (12:1-3)

With "now concerning" (v. 1) Paul introduces a new area of discussion; a discussion that is of vital importance to him. He wishes his readers to be knowledgeable and understanding, not ignorant, in the matters that follow.

Paul reminds his readers of what they used to be, "Gentiles," heathens, pagans, not Christians; men following dumb idols, especially when contrasted with the Holy Spirit. They were helpless, for they were "carried away" by their worship to these dead idols. Every path these men followed seemed to lead to idol worship.

But Paul also makes a comparison between their former heathen state and their present Christian state (v. 3). A Christian at all times acknowledges the lordship of Jesus Christ. That principle here applies especially to speaking "in the Spirit," glossolalia. Speaking in tongues honors God (14:2) and Romans 10:9 does not seem to be under consideration. It is possible that someone under ecstatic influence may have cried, "Jesus is accursed," and because of the excitement under which the statement was made, some were tempted to believe this came from God. But this is contrary to the Christian attitude, for it denies the lordship of Christ. An utterance under the influence of the Holy Spirit is different; it asserts the lordship of Christ. If it does involve glossolalia, it would also have to involve interpretation (or prophecy) for the statement to be understood publicly.

D. The Unity in Diverse Spirituals (Manifestations) (12:4-11)

Having laid down this cornerstone, Paul enlarges his discussion to cover "spirituals."

These manifestations of the Holy Spirit (or "gifts," as the KJV rather inaccurately describes them) have both unity and variety (vv. 4-6). These have not the same purpose or magnitude, but each is given by one and the same Holy Spirit. We shall use the popular term *gifts*, but the idea of gift lies in their quality and ground. These, like salvation, are a work of grace, but they still reside, as we shall see, in the Holy Spirit. In other words, their presence in someone does not necessarily signify great holiness or

106

sanctification. "Diversities" gives the idea of distribution and (as is made clear throughout) this is done by the choice of the Spirit.

Administrations also differ according to God's decisions. These refer to the functions and services of those having the "gifts." "Ministrations" *(ASV)* indicates the purpose of spiritual manifestations; these are for the help and strengthening of the Church. It is a useful service. It is, however, the same Lord who is served.

Operations are also diversified; these workings revealing both the availability and the effect of divine power. They result from gifts and ministrations and are workings in virtue of the power operative therein. But again it is the same God, as the context shows, that "worketh all [things] in all [people]." Notice the strong Trinitarian bent in "Spirit," "Lord" (which is generally Christ in Paul's writings), and "God."

These gifts are given for the purpose of spiritual profit (v. 7). *Manifestation* is a vital word, for it clarifies the meaning of "gift" and helps to properly define this entire section. On the basis of context, it appears as a subjective genitive and means to make evident to the understanding by proof. It is a shining forth, as light makes manifest. The exercise of the gifts makes His presence evident. Remember this is a "manifestation of the *Spirit*" and not a manifestation of a gift. He is the Source, and in Him these *charismi* reside. The result is worship, not admiration of the gift. The ultimate purpose is that all the Church may profit. On this basis we might add that the gifts are as needed now as they were then.

Having explained these important foundational concepts, Paul proceeds to list nine particular manifestations of the Spirit (vv. 8-10). Wisdom by itself includes practical skill in the affairs of life, and in particular in the things of Christ and God's will. First Corinthians 2 may be an example. It is action on the basis of knowledge. It is the ability to see how to handle a particular situation as the Holy Spirit directs. Paul uses "word" here to qualify wisdom for a purpose. This would include speaking or uttering wisdom and, in some cases, even teaching. But "word" also limits this operation. This gift, as is true of the other gifts, is relegated to time and place, to beginning and end. The fruit of the Spirit, in Galatians 5:22, 23, have a beginning but in a particular way no ending, for they are intended to grow within us

107

indefinitely. However, the gifts have a particular setting in which to operate, for they are manifestations of the Holy Spirit.

For example, a church meeting is in debate because two sides are arguing and no one can come up with a practical solution to settle the difficulty. Someone stands up who, under the direction of the Holy Spirit, offers a "word of wisdom" which shows the way to an answer. The gift operates in a particular setting; being manifested by the Holy Spirit who dwells within the Spirit-filled believer. At another time, the Holy Spirit may manifest himself again in such a necessary manner. Thus all profit.[145]

The second manifestation listed is the "word of knowledge." Pearlman defined this as supernaturally inspired utterance of facts.[146] This could include fundamental principles of the Word and the Christian religion. It would include a measure of understanding of the great facts of life and the universe as they are known to God,[147] a knowledge of God which can be dispensed,[148] and a knowledge of happenings.[149]

Wisdom and knowledge differ in that knowledge involves insight, whereas wisdom is the application of that insight and understanding to a particular matter; the application of principle to practice. Wisdom builds with material that knowledge has provided and uses it profitably. ("Word" has already been discussed.)

Throughout this list, no item carries the definite article, which fastens the eye on the quality and source of the gift rather than on its individuality.

The third item on this list is faith. Faith is infinite trust and belief in God, His promises, and His faithfulness. But this gift seems to have special emphasis in that "it would seem to come upon certain of God's servants in times of special crisis or opportunity in such mighty power that they are lifted right out of the realm of even natural or ordinary faith in God—and have a divine certainty put within their souls that triumphs over everything. . . ."[150] It is different from ordinary faith which is a disposition. It may be what Christ is talking about in Matthew 17:20. Notice that faith as a gift is a manifestation of power, while faith as a fruit is a quality of character. Weymouth calls it "special faith" and examples may be 1 Kings 18:30-46 and Acts 3:1-10. This

108

faith flows out in demonstration, advancing the Church and its work.

It might be well to note again that the gifts work together by (the) one Spirit. For example, the gift of faith may set free a gift of healing. Of course, the first prerequisite is to be filled with the Holy Spirit.

The next item is "gifts of healing." This may mean that different kinds of diseases need different kinds of healing, such as is included in Matthew 10:1. This is generally a very positive gift(s). It is used of God in supernaturally ministering health to the sick through prayer. It seems to be a sign-gift and is greatly involved in the work of evangelism.[151] It should not be understood, however, that this means power to heal everyone. We must take into account the sovereignty of God and the unbelief of man. It must also be considered that not every healing is the result of the gifts of healings.[152] The sick are not totally dependent on one used in this area or gift. It seems to be the most frequently displayed of the power gifts.

"Working of miracles" is another addition to this list. A miracle is an orderly intervention in the regular operations of nature; a supernatural suspension of a natural law. The phrase translated is "works of power."[153] There is a distinction between faith and miracles, and a distinction between healings and miracles. Miracles may be negative and destructive as well as positive. Healing is always positive. Note also that all miracles are not the result of faith or the gift of miracles, but are due to the sovereign work of God.[154]

Biblical prophecy may be by revelation, wherein the prophet proclaims a message previously received through a dream, a vision, or the Word of the Lord. Or it may be ecstatic, inspirational utterance on the spur of the moment. There are many scriptural examples of both forms. Ecstatic, inspirational prophecy may take the form of exaltation and worship of Christ, or hortatory admonition, or inspirational comfort and encouragement to the saints.[155]

It has both a broad sense of general knowledge and a specific sense of special knowledge (messages). This particular gift, which includes forthtelling as well as foretelling, undoubtedly has the narrower sense.

109

The purpose of this gift of prophecy is threefold.[156] It is intended to edify and upbuild, add new material and strengthen old, and instruct and improve spiritually. It is intended to exhort or to incite by argument or advice and to give warnings or advice. This gift is also given to offer comfort and strength, and to assist, support, and console in trouble or worry.[157]

Prediction in prophecy is not precisely stated in 1 Corinthians 14, but is inherent in the prophet's ministry.[158] Thus, it may be included in prophecy. It is a clear command of the Word of God that prophecy (and the other utterance gifts) must be judged.[159] Error may be included or the message may come from the wrong source (which will be discussed under the discerning of spirits).

As far as prophecy and preaching are concerned, we must admit that prophecy is sometimes involved in preaching, but generally the gift and the administration are somewhat different in that prophecy is the result of spontaneous spiritual inspiration, while preaching is the result of the study of existing revelation. At times, however, the two are combined.

Should these messages be in the first person? This question has been the source of controversy among Pentecostal believers. Generally because of method, third person would seem most reasonable. Man does not become a passive mouthpiece but God quickens his spirit to speak His message even though it be beyond natural ability and understanding to do so.[160]

"Discerning of spirits" is the policeman and protector of the group. There are three sources of operation: (1) the divine Holy Spirit, (2) demons, and (3) the human spirit or flesh. This gift enables one to discern a person's spiritual character and the source of his actions and messages. It is the safeguard of the gifts. However, it must be distinguished from natural insight or a faultfinding spirit.[161] This gift is supported by two other tests: 1 John 4:1-6 lists a doctrinal test and Matthew 7:15-23, a practical test. There are numerous New Testament examples.[162]

"Kinds of tongues" is defined as the power to speak by the Holy Spirit in a language the speaker has not learned; the message being understood by the hearers through the operation of the gift of interpretation. This gift and that of interpretation must also be judged by spiritual quality and scriptural correctness. There is an acknowledged difference between tongues as the evidence of the baptism in the Holy Spirit and in individual praying, and tongues as a gift (as here used).[163] The difference is basically one of purpose: one is to edify one's own spirit; the other is to edify the congregation.

Why could we not be content with prophecy alone? God has not so ordained it. Tongues, even as the gift, does serve as a sign [164] and Paul lists it as a viable ministry.[165]

"Tongues" and the "interpretation of tongues" are almost like one gift; they are so closely connected. The latter gift renders inspired public messages in tongues understandable to the general listening audience by repeating them in the language of the hearers. Again, there must be judgment by the congregation regarding quality and content.

Once more Paul makes his theme stand out (v. 11). These are gifts of the one Holy Spirit. He distributes to each individual as He wills and chooses. The choice is His and the glory is God's.

E. The Individuality of One Body (12:12-31)

As Paul considers the operation of these manifestations of the Spirit within the Church, he is moved to think of the operation of the Church itself. As he does so, Paul realizes that the great analogy of the Church is the body; one body with many functions. His thinking thus carries him to consider the Church as the body of Christ. In that vein he proceeds. He begins with a comparison between the physical body and this spiritual Body. The body is single, but has many parts (vv. 12, 13). These various parts cannot be separated from one body. The same is true of Christ's body. We have to suppose that "Christ" here means the body of Christ, for the person of Christ is not divided.

We are initiated into Christ's body "by one Spirit" or "in one Spirit" (ASV). Some see this as referring to water baptism and the washing of regeneration. While it may be speaking of something of which water baptism is a symbol, it is the work of the Spirit that makes the difference. Incorporation does not depend on the administration of baptism, but the working of the Spirit. Some say that the Spirit is not the agent. But He cannot be the element of baptism here because the body of Christ is. Thus it has to mean

111

"in virtue of His operation." This would make the phrase "by one Spirit" a dative of instrumentality rather than a dative of location.

This work is accomplished regardless of station. "Jews or Greeks" (v. 13, *ASV*) probably refers to nationality and birth. "Bond or free" refers to rank or position. These have been made to "drink of one Spirit" *(ASV)*. Some see a reference to Communion; others a reference to the baptism in the Holy Spirit.[166] Certainly we have to say it carries with it a unity, close contact, and fellowship in figurative language.

This body which has been so established has many members, each of which is necessary and important (vv. 14-20). This diversity in unity is illustrated in several ways. Paul uses the illustration of the foot and the hand. The foot might feel inadequate in comparison with the dexterity of the hand. But the foot has a function that is vital; therefore, it is important to and part of the body. Paul's question here requires a positive answer.

Paul also uses the illustration of the ear and the eye. Again inadequacy and a feeling of inferiority might be problems, but that should not be so. Paul argues that if the whole body were one member such as an eye or an ear, then the body would not really be a body; for certain functions and members necessary for a body would be absent—thus, no body. Each question demands a positive and self-asserted answer. Paul then gives the solution to and source of diversity within the body. God does with it as He pleases, since He knows best. We are thus returned to verse 11 and a recurring theme. This is a further strike against division and strife; there is diversity and individuality yet unity in one body.

Thus the individual members must respect one another (vv. 21-26). Again we see the illustrations of eye and hand, and head and feet. The eye is a long-range "high" member; the hand is a close-at-work member; but the eye in its visionary work cannot reject the hand's menial working. The head, on top, cannot despise the feet, on the bottom. ("Hand" is singular and generally refers to the right hand or main hand. "Feet" is plural for they do not have such a dominant one.)

There must be a mutual respect and honor of lesser members. "Feeble" (delicate but vital) organs must be cared for. "Less honorable" members are given more honor because we give them special care and clothe them. "Uncomely parts," within the framework of the analogy, may refer to organs of procreation and excretion. Whether this is true or not, there are more and less attractive parts probably because of function. But each has a place and honor in the body. Each member must receive equal honor and care, for God ordained the bodily operations as they are and He has evened out the gaining and receiving of honor. This was done to prevent division and splits in the body and to promote concern among the members for each other. Thus sorrow is shared, as well as joy and honor.

Paul has been using the example of the body to illustrate his point; now he directly applies what he has said to the Corinthians. Paul probably has in mind the local church because of the absence of the definite article in the Greek in verse 27. Here as elsewhere there is individuality in unity. All of these workers are called and ordained by God.

But what about the order here? Does listing these in importance (vv. 27-31) tear down what Paul has said about equality? "Here the order is not determined by the essential nature of the gifts as allied to the intellect or will or feelings but by the relative importance of the gifts in the work and edification of the Church."[167] It should be noted that Paul begins by listing persons and then gifts or items, so it is difficult to carry a list of importance too far. Also, we must observe that men do not choose; God distributes.

"Apostles" were chief ministers entrusted with the powers necessary to found the Church and make an entire revelation of God's will.[168] They were certainly authoritative witnesses to the fact of the gospel and especially to the Resurrection. With "prophets," Paul seems to have in mind a settled office rather than an "occasional" manifestation. We have to add that their work included inspired speech. They seemed enabled by the Holy Spirit to prophesy, interpret Scripture, and write by inspiration. "Teachers" labored in word and doctrine with or without a pastoral charge. The word itself lends us some help. They play(ed) an important role due to the extremely high cost of hand-copied books. It appears that in some cases this ministry was local.[169]

113

With "then" (v. 28), Paul transfers from people to gifts. Miracles, healings, and tongues have already been discussed. "Helps" is an unlisted ministry elsewhere. It appears to be those who had compassion and ministry to the sick, weak, or helpless in some fashion. Special persons without set office may have rendered special assistance in needy cases. There are those who parallel "he that giveth" (Romans 12:8) with "helps," and "he that ruleth" (Romans 12:8) with governments. Some have stated that this could not be a general work for all in the church due to its list among the gifts. This has a degree of truth, but in another sense the other "gifts" are also available to all according to the will of the Spirit. "Governments" is somewhat unfamiliar, but it had to do with some type of higher department of ministration. In a comparison with 1 Timothy 5:17, it may have involved elders who did not labor in word and doctrine, but who were charged with some form of leadership and distribution.

The questions of verses 29 and 30 must admit a "no" answer each time. Paul is intending to hammer home diversity not exclusiveness. It must be remembered it is the Spirit who distributes as He wishes and manifests as He chooses. It should also be noted that on the basis of the context, "speak with tongues" refers to the gift not the evidence of the baptism in the Holy Spirit.

Paul concludes by urging his readers to "covet . . . the best gifts." How is this determined and does it mean one gift is worth more than others? The criterion of worth is use; purpose determines value. Those most serviceable to others are the most valuable; and thus the greater or best gifts. Ultimately, those are to be most desired that will bring God the greatest glory in the situation and time and edify the Church to the largest and most practical degree. This naturally leads to that "more excellent way." Paul does not abolish gifts; he just shows the environment in which they are to exist and the force by which they are to be guided. That environment and force is love.

F. The Ground of Love (13:1-13)

Drummond called love the *summum bonum;* the supreme good. It comes from and is at best a part of God. "Love is more than a characteristic of God, it is His character." John wrote:

To you whom I love I say, let us go on loving one another, for love comes from God. Every man who truly loves is God's son and has some knowledge of him. But the man who does not love cannot know him at all, for God is love (1 John 4:7, 8, *Phillips*).

Love is thus spoken of and discussed in numerous texts of the Word of God. But never does it reach a loftier position than here, nor does any word seem so inadequate in comparison as here. Robertson and Plummer cite Harnack as speaking of this chapter as "the greatest, strongest, deepest thing Paul ever wrote."[170] Paul places it here to teach the Corinthians that all knowledge, the gifts of the Spirit, and anything else must always have the ground of love, or they become "nothing." As he wrote, Paul surely had his eye on Jesus.

Paul immediately establishes the supremacy of love (vv. 1-3). Love is supreme over "tongues" and speech. No language in heaven or earth can be compared with the practice of love. Thus, the art of oratory, which was highly valued at Corinth, is set in its proper place. "Brass" denotes first metal, copper, and then any object made from it. Here it probably refers to a gong. "Sounding" might be rendered "resounding." Knox translates "sounding brass" as "echoing bronze." "Tinkling" is rather "clashing," like the sound of heavy cymbals. The speech or sound may be attractive, enticing, entertaining, and enchanting; it may be alluring and compelling, demonstrative and persuasive. But if it is not motivated by love and done within the atmosphere of love, it is only noise, "sound without soul."

Love is supreme to great knowledge and understanding. This involves inspiration and prophecy; the work of the seer. Mysteries are here known—truths that men could never learn and penetrate for themselves—but only because it pleased God to reveal them. "All" denotes the extent of this knowledge. Such knowledge without love is nothing.

Love is superior to great faith. The indication is of faith that moves mountain after mountain. Without love as the ground, even such miracle-working faith as this is of no value.

Love reigns over great generosity of goods and self. There may be generosity to the point of beggary and yet involve an absence of love. Men of the first century, as today, commonly saw great merit in deeds of charity and suffering. Paul rejects these on their

115

own merit alone. Love must be the ground and motive. This giving may have stubbornness, pride, or display behind it. If I gave myself as a martyr, which is the furthest this could go, if love was not the point, then there would be no gain of any kind.

Love is supreme in its position and practical in its display (vv. 4-7). Love has great patience toward evil and kindly activity in good. It "suffereth long" or is long-suffering.[171] It has an infinite capacity for endurance and patience with people. Love is "kind."[172] It shows goodness toward those who ill treat it. It gives itself in the service of others. It "envieth not."[173] This includes jealousy. It has no petty feelings toward those, for instance, who are doing the same work only better. Love is not displeased at the success of others. Love "vaunteth not" itself. The root of the word points to a "windbag." It is "not puffed up." Humility is an ingredient of love.[174] The Pharisees had a false humility and so were afraid to go to God; thus, they went to angels (Colossians 2:18, 19).

Love is concerned with giving itself rather than asserting itself. It does not "behave itself unseemly." This carries the idea of anything disgraceful, dishonorable, or indiscreet. Love is not discourteous.[175] Instead, it is the source of true etiquette. Love "seeketh not her own."[176] This is a central point in the discussion. Love is totally unselfish. Further, it is "not easily provoked."[177] Phillips translates this, "It is not touchy." It "thinketh no evil." It imputes no evil to anyone nor holds anything against anyone. *Thinketh* is a word Paul uses frequently for the reckoning or imputing of righteousness to the believers. Here it is connected with the keeping of accounts, noting them down, and reckoning them to someone. Love takes no account of evil. It is guileless.[178]

Love "rejoiceth in the truth."[179] Even love cannot rejoice when the truth is denied. It rejoices in the gospel. It "beareth all things."[180] It endures without disclosing to the world its stress or complaint. There is no bragging. Webster includes, "To hold back; refrain patiently: To withhold anger or reproach." It "believeth all things." With a good conscience it puts good to another's credit. In trust and faith it believes the very best it honestly can at all times. If "believeth" is impossible, then "hopeth" comes to the fore. This involves the refusal to take failure as final. If someone is not what he should be, then love hopes and prays for his improvement. This confidence looks to the ultimate triumph of the grace of God. It trusts for good even when others have stopped. When evil is seen it hopes for recovery. Love "endureth all things." This involves steadfastness even in difficult circumstances. Endurance and fortitude in the battle show forth. There is the presence of a patient, loving spirit.[181]

This love shall endure forever (vv. 8-13). It is compared with prophecy, tongues, and knowledge. They are all in a sense "temporary." They shall cease or pass away in view of the total Perfection. That painfully acquired knowledge of earthly things will vanish away in light of the overwhelming knowledge of God. That day, which has not yet come, is fast approaching. Prophesying in part probably means God does not reveal everything so that even the prophet has but a partial glimpse of truth; his prophecy is accurate but incomplete. These all are a part of what we shall know in full when we stand before God.

To explain, Paul uses the illustration of a child becoming a man (v. 11). "Put away" is an indication of the determination on Paul's part not to be ruled by childish attitudes. The tense is perfect, which shows that Paul put away childish things with decision and finality. He also uses the illustration of the mirror reflection (v. 12). Mirrors were a specialty of Corinth; but they were made of polished brass so the image was dim. Silvering glass was not discovered until the 13th century. Here on earth our sight of eternal things is at best indistinct. Moulton does an excellent job on this verse: "Now I am acquiring knowledge which is only partial at best: then I shall have learnt my lesson, shall know, as God in my mortal life knew me."[182]

This love stands above faith and hope, both of which are essential in the plan and work of salvation. These three items are often linked in the New Testament,[183] all being of great merit. But love will not fail or "fall" in the sense of cessation. There are actually two distinct ways of looking at this. It may be faith will be superseded by sight, and hope by fruition, but love will just keep growing. Thus faith and hope will only abide with love "now," or in the present. Or it may be that Paul puts these three on the same footing in respect to enduringness, with love being greater not more lasting. New objects of trust and desire will come into sight in the widening visions of life eternal.[184] Accordingly then, love surpasses its companions, being the character of God. In love is the fruition of faith's efforts and hope's anticipations.

Certainly love is made the greatest; it is only fitting then that love is the last word of the chapter. It is truly the last word! As we grow in God we see and understand more of God in love. The need of today is still for love. The heart needs love and the Christian must allow every thought, action, and attitude to be ruled and motivated by this, which is the greatest of all in any life, the ground of love.

G. The Excellence of (Prophecy in) Edification (14:1-19)

This is the concluding chapter in Paul's discussion of public worship. He has led up to this chapter with his declaration of the operation and gifts of the Holy Spirit (12:1-11); his analogy of the Church as the body of Christ (12:12-31); and his great chapter on the ground and motivation of everything and everyone within the Church—love (13:1-13). Now he is prepared to make an analysis of the utterance gifts—tongues and prophecy.

Paul makes a very strong case for prophecy here. This has led some to deny he supported the operation of "tongues" at all, and thus the modern-day "tongues movement" has been criticized. However, there are certain considerations that must be made before we examine this chapter further. There was tremendous pride among the Corinthians over their use of tongues. They were being "used" in the wrong manner; there had been a neglect of the other gifts of the Spirit, perhaps because they were not as flashy; this had created a degeneration of spiritual good in the public worship services. Paul intended to correct this.

Further, Paul is not speaking of the evidence of tongues following the infilling with the Holy Spirit, but of the use of tongues by one already filled with the Spirit and the gift of tongues. Paul is not abolishing tongues and their use. He clearly states that he does much such speaking (14:18) and he urges others to do likewise (14:5). But he does set tongues in proper perspective. Finally, we must remember the major theme here—edification in utterance. All things must be beneficial, must be guided by the Spirit, and must be edifying to the Church.

Paul links us to the ground of all Christian actions—love; joins us again with his discussion of 12:31; and introduces his discussion of prophecy. He writes, "Follow after love" (v. 1, *ASV*). Love is not to be pursued to the neglect of anything else but in the interest of all else. This is a continuous activity, a continual pursuit. There is a constant need and requirement that everything be done out of love.

And we are to "desire spiritual gifts." *Desire* is the same word translated "covet earnestly" in 12:31. It is proper and good to desire these spiritual gifts (as listed in 12:8-10, in particular). They should be earnestly sought within the framework of love. Some have concluded that "follow after" is directed to the entire congregation and "desire" to certain ones in the congregation.[185] But the language of the verse does not convey this. Every believer is to be Spirit-filled; therefore, any Spirit-filled believer might manifest these spiritual gifts.

Yet Paul places an emphasis on prophecy. He is doing so because its use here is most edifying for the congregation. He is not setting up a list of highest and lowest gifts, because the gifts are resident in the Holy Spirit who is resident in the believer. But we must remember the Corinthians' overemphasis of tongues. Paul wants to reassert a proper balance and show what is most edifying, and why, in the situation.

An explanation follows (v. 2). Paul first explains the action and communion of tongues.[186] The clear reason for his admonition is that while there is adequate sound in "tongues," there is no sense. "Tongues" do not edify anyone else because no one can understand what is being said. Only God understands. "Not unto men" shows that, whatever the intention, the man still speaks only to God. "In the spirit," on the basis of the context and verses 14, 15, may refer to the believer's spirit which is quickened and sanctified by the Holy Spirit. It is possible to speak "in the spirit" without the aid of the understanding. A mystery is spoken. Deep things are uttered that should be rationally spoken and understood. This revelation should be known, but here it stops short of disclosure and merely teases the listeners. And the public assembly under these circumstances is not the place for such "private" communion, unless the gift of interpretation is also in operation; otherwise, the result is a notable lack of edification.

Prophecy in this situation will result in edification, exhortation,

119

and comfort (v. 3). "Unto men" implies that love has led to the proper result. Such prophecy has the following results: upbuilding, teaching, and help. "Comfort" makes reference to sorrow and fear, and is found only here in the New Testament. "Exhortation" makes reference to duty; "edification" to knowledge, character, and the progress of the Church.

Paul explains that "tongues" are for personal edification and therefore have value, but prophecy edifies to a greater extent because it edifies the whole church (v. 4). Speaking in a tongue is edifying to the speaker himself. In what way? It is an exercise of the spirit in conjunction with the Holy Spirit, Godward. And in such communion one's spirit is blessed and edified. The edification of prophecy is along the lines mentioned in verses 3 and 4.

The writer summarizes what he has said by establishing the good of tongues but the greater good of prophecy in this situation (or the combination of tongues and interpretation), because of the edification the church assembly receives from an understandable message (v. 5). In so doing, Paul adds another reason for the excellence of prophecy. The speaker of prophecy is a "greater" person than the speaker in tongues—unless the latter interprets his ecstatic utterance. Tongues plus interpretation accomplishes in two steps what prophecy accomplishes in one, but Paul places them on equal footing, for the same end is accomplished—edification for the body of gathered believers. A general principle is clear: The gifts of the Spirit are intended for the edification of the members of the body of Christ.

Paul uses a series of illustrations to show the profit given to the Church by issuing forth certain, understandable words and messages. He makes reference to those forms that carry clear messages (v. 6). We must again remember Paul is not abandoning the use of "tongues," but placing it in proper perspective. Note the term "brethren," indicating his close relationship to the Corinthian believers.

Paul uses himself as an illustration ("if I come . . ."). The difficulty with his coming to minister to them "speaking with tongues" would be what has already been discussed in 14:2-4. It would be impossible for the congregation to understand the message (except by interpretation); therefore, it would be profitless to the church. What help could he be to his troubled readers if he brought a sound that could not be understood? Rather, Paul adds, it is necessary for such profit that there be revelation or knowledge, or prophesying or doctrine. The second pair matches the first pair. Revelation is ministered by the prophet; knowledge is ministered by the teacher. Revelation relates in a narrow sense to specific matters. (For knowledge, see 12:8.) Prophesying speaks of giving utterance to that which has been revealed. Doctrine involves instruction in the Christian faith. All four are clearly linked. And all four are distinct from "tongues" (if the "tongues" are without an interpretation) because they are spoken in an understandable manner.

Paul draws another illustration from the inanimate world (v. 7). There is a reference to music. "Pipe" is a flute and represents the wind instruments. "Harp" (from which we get guitar) represents the stringed instruments.[187] A melody rightly played will speak to the very heart of man. But for this to be accomplished there must be a variety of harmony, expression, and chord. Without this there is aimless, profitless jangle. Sound must communicate meaning and message.

From the inanimate world Paul also draws the illustration of the battle trumpet (v. 8). In the days before modern mechanized and electronic warfare, the trumpet played an important part. One melody was for reveille; another for taps; another for advance in battle; another for retreat. If there was no clear distinction of sound, there would be no resultant understanding among the troops. Then who would prepare for the battle? The answer: No one!

From the living world, Paul adds yet another illustration, and implies application to the situation at Corinth (v. 9). "Likewise ye" means "take a lesson here"; understand and apply it. "By the tongue" appears to refer to the physical tongue (setting this verse in marked contrast to the lifeless realm of vv. 7, 8). Paul seems to have other than the supernatural "tongue" in mind. What is true with the inanimate is true to a larger degree with the human tongue; it articulates as it is directed. And this was the problem at Corinth. The words had no meaning; they were not "intelligible" (RSV). They were speaking "into the air." This proverbial expression notes ineffectiveness and profitlessness.

In his last illustration, Paul summarizes all he has been pointing

121

to (v. 10). He draws from the widest possible source: "in the world." There are literally thousands of dialects and sounds in the world. Goodspeed translates this verse: "There are probably ever so many different languages in the world." None of these is without "signification." Paul asserts that each voice carries the real nature of a voice. In other words, it means something to somebody.

Paul makes it clear that there must be an existing understanding between speaker and listener, or each will view the other as a "barbarian" (v. 11). "Meaning" carries the thought of "force" or "power." Speech is a persuasive and communicative force. But speech that is not understood is not; it is powerless, futile, and useless. The listener may hear, but try as he may he cannot understand. The speaker may repeat his message, but he cannot make his listener understand. It is as Paul writes in 14:2, "He speaketh mysteries." The result is each considers the other a "barbarian." The Greeks divided the world into Greeks and barbarians. While Paul had in mind primarily unintelligent speech and the lack of communication, the fuller sense of the term *barbarian* (one beyond the limits of civilization) is implied. What a tragic ending to something filled with promise and value!

The application of these illustrations is made to the Corinthians (v. 12). "Even so ye" indicates the need to understand and apply these ideas to their situation. The Corinthians were coveters of these spiritual gifts; they desired to see them manifested in the congregation. They had an enthusiastic zeal and ardent desire which was good as long as the aim was the profit of others. Unfortunately, the Corinthians did not always act out of the best motives or to the best purposes. They thought too little of the Source of these gifts and too much of their outward appearance and expression. Again and again Paul speaks from his great pastoral heart: Edify the church; excel in the gifts of the Spirit for the edification of the church.

Having said this, Paul makes his point on the immediate subject of the use of "tongues" (v. 13). If the church is to be edified by an "unknown" tongue, they must understand what is said. Therefore, the admonition is to pray for the interpretation. There was nothing static about these spiritual gifts. A man who was used in the gift of tongues might also be used in another gift; such as interpretation. It was to this end that he should pray; again, to edify the church.

Verse 14 is tied in with what has preceded, for Paul explains further why one should pray to interpret what he has spoken in a tongue and, at the same time, he establishes the need for understanding and the place of "tongues" and prophecy. Paul speaks in the first person singular, stating general possibility not actuality (note v. 19), perhaps to make the admonition less disagreeable. "Spirit" refers to a man's spirit. It is contrasted with "understanding." At salvation the human spirit is regenerated and renewed by the Holy Spirit. The understanding is also changed. But in the area of gifts, particularly tongues, the understanding may not be used by the changed spirit. This is a difficult thing to understand, perhaps even a mystery.

Normally man works through his understanding. But in "tongues" this is not so. And this is where the problem arises. One's "spirit" does not communicate the clear messages with another's spirit that one's "understanding" does with another's understanding. Now he that prays and speaks in a tongue does well. But because the understanding is not used, it is incomprehensible to anyone else. Paul is not calling for barren intellectualism, but he is discrediting assumption made in the name of "the Spirit" that denounces sober and sound judgment. He shall do so even more directly presently.

How then stands the matter? (v. 15). Paul answers by calling attention to two activities: praying and singing. The singing is of praise to God, perhaps even using the psalms. Paul indicates that he will do both—pray and sing "with the spirit" and "with the understanding." There is a place and value to both. While the primary reference is probably to public worship, these activities are not resigned to public worship alone. Paul recognizes the gift of tongues and the value of understandable speech. Therefore, he will do that which will edify the body of Christ. In this context and situation, that means he will interpret his "tongue" when in a public gathering in order to follow that rule of edification. He will do what is most expedient and edifying to the church at all times.

Paul sets the picture of what would happen if the understanding was not involved in the public worship (vv. 16, 17). Lack of learning and edification would result. "Unlearned" denotes a private individual. There are examples of the use of this word for laymen as opposed to priests; private citizens as opposed to public officials; men without military rank as opposed to officers. What then does Paul mean by one who is "unlearned"? Some have concluded he means a non-Christian. Yet verses 23, 24 seem to distinguish between "unlearned" and "unbelieving." Some claim the word denotes ignorant or unskilled. Others have objected that in verse 23, he is distinguished from the whole church; therefore, he cannot be a Christian.

But the unlearned is not so clearly distinguished from the "whole church." And declaring the presence of God is not just a mark of conversion (see v. 25). This word was used in some religious associations to denote nonmembers who were allowed to participate in the sacrifices. And from this some have concluded that Paul means those who were interested, but had not yet committed themselves to Christianity.[188] Either of the last two possibilities is reasonable. Clearly this man was unlearned in the matter at hand.

There may be blessing and thanksgiving in the public worship service. Nonetheless, the unlearned cannot say "amen" to the blessing of the Spirit because he cannot understand it. "Amen" was used as a congregational response to prayers and carries that idea here. The worshiper thereby makes the prayer of another his own. A note of agreement and assent is sounded. But the unlearned cannot do this because he does not know what the prayer said. Others would have the same problem, but there was special concern for the unlearned. There is nothing wrong with the prayer. "Thou . . . givest thanks well" (v. 17), but there is no edification because there is no understanding.

As he concludes his point, Paul restresses the place of tongues and prophecy, and their relationship. He returns to the use of the first person singular (vv. 18, 19). This exercise of speaking in tongues was widespread at Corinth. Yet Paul acknowledges that he exercises it to an even greater extent. Far from decrying it, he thanks God for it because it comes by the Holy Spirit for the aid and strength of the individual.

But Paul adds a condition or exception concerning what should properly take place in the church assembly. Again the theme is edification. Some of the Corinthians gloried in their ability to speak in a "tongue." But Paul could and did speak more than they. Yet he stresses above all that which is most serviceable on the occasion. Paul's thought is how best to benefit his brethren in the Lord, and the listener. In this case, that means speaking in an understandable language because that is how the listener is taught. Always, and above all, there is that overriding need for edification.

H. The Excellence (of Prophecy) in Spiritual Persuasion (14:20-25)

Paul points out another major reason for the excellence of prophecy in the public assembly. This had to do with spiritual persuasion, or the conviction to even the most skeptical that God is truly present. This, after all, should be the aim of everything done and said in the church—to see men convicted of their sin and immaturity and persuaded of the power of God in Christ to transform and mature them.

With neatness and precision Paul links the previous section with this one (v. 20). He appeals to the good sense of his readers. He directs them to understanding and maturity. There seemed to be an almost childish delight by the Corinthians in tongues. But Paul wants them to act like men and do what is excellent and edifying. "In understanding" reflects reasoning. It means "midriff" or "diaphragm," for this is where the Greeks located thought. It indicates not only the thinking mind, but also the heart, as the seat of emotions; the complete man, who is filled with something; and covers the direction of a person's life.[189] The rebuke is tempered by "brethren."

However, in malice or wrong they should be children. There is an innocence and directness of affection in a babe. This innocence, simplicity, and distaste for evil should be clear always. But they should have the minds of men. Paul has described the existing situation in the first part of the verse, but with "howbeit" he describes what he desires to see.

From the Old Testament Paul draws a fact that his readers had apparently not considered (v. 21). He condenses and adapts Isaiah 28:11, 12. "Law" in Jewish usage extended to Scripture at

125

large and the Old Testament in general. Within the context of Isaiah, the text is applied as follows: The Israelites were mocking God and His teaching through His prophet, as though it were only suitable for infants. God in anger and retribution threatens therefore to give His lessons through the lips and speech of the Assyrians, and therefore to spell out ruin. Paul sees a principle here. The "tongues" may serve the same purpose as the Assyrian speech. It may *confirm* in unbelief rather than convicting of unbelief. Even with Israel there was the presence of mercy. God desired to use the Assyrians to return the Israelites to himself. Yet the Lord said they would not hear and would continue in their unbelief.

"Wherefore" indicates a conclusion and application of what has just been said (v. 22). These tongues are for a sign to the unbeliever; to him who refuses to hear until he finds his unbelief confirmed and justified by this phenomenon of "tongues." This does not seem to indicate any real type of saving sign, due to the close connection of verses 21, 22, and Paul's desire to dull the Corinthians' "delight" for tongues. This is not the effect on the believer however.

On the other hand, prophecy has a very positive effect. It could really be called a sign of grace. It will lead to salvation and belief. Since it is easily understood, it tends to convict, convince, and change toward belief and praise of God. It is for believers. Notice that it is God who speaks in both ways. And it is the appeal, taste, condition, and response of the hearer that makes the final difference in outcome.

Paul details what he means by what he has just written (v. 23). He visualizes the whole congregation gathering and all speaking in tongues. An unbeliever or one unlearned walks in, and not understanding or seeing the spiritual sense in the scene, feels justified in declaring these Christians mad. (Note that it says "into one place." This is a support for the regular Lord's Day services and regular attendance at them.)

If, as the Corinthians thought, tongues is the highest gift of the Spirit, then nothing could be better than to have the whole church speaking "with tongues." But the result is not what they had expected, but is in keeping with the intention stated in verses 21, 22. There is a marked lack of edification toward the unlearned or unbelieving who come in, and they claim madness and irrationality on the part of the Christians. This pushes them away from the Church, rather than drawing them into its fellowship.

The effects of prophecy are in clear contrast to this (vv. 24, 25). The direct, understandable message from God will have very powerful results. The "outsider" will be "convinced of all." This means the man will be convicted; the prophetic word will show him his condition and state. He will be "judged of all." This phrase means to put on trial to sift judicially; to examine by question after penetrating question. The Word of the Lord throws a searchlight into hidden recesses. The man will realize then, through the work of the Holy Spirit, that he is guilty of sin and stands under the judgment of God. The secrets of his heart will be made manifest. That which he thought safely hidden in some deep recess of his own being shall be brought to light. "Made manifest" may carry a double meaning. Perhaps some particular sin is made mention of, or the unlearned or unbelieving may see an image of himself in the general prophecy on sin. In these cases, the sin may be manifested to the congregation or simply to the individual.

Generally, there appears first the inward work (vv. 24, 25), then the outward product. First comes the penetration of the Law, the measuring stick of righteousness, morality, and justice. Then comes the gospel with its presentation of mercy, faith, and grace. The results are both worship and witness. The last part of verse 25 is reminiscent of Isaiah 45:14. So powerful will be the effect of the divine message and presence that the unbeliever will prostrate himself before God. There will be humility, confession, and surrender, as the man worships God. He will praise, rejoice, and realize the lordship of Christ. The once unbelieving, but now believing man will leave the congregation announcing, "God is in you." Such a church is successful. To have the Holy Spirit so working is the sign of a healthy, vigorous church, the body of Christ.

I. The Excellence of Order in the Church Assembly (Concerning Utterance) (14:26-33)

It has already been established that Paul's purpose in what he writes is for the salvation and edification of others. He continues along the same line of thought. In applying the principle of edification, he deals with the difficult subject of order in the church assembly, in particular with regard to these spiritual utterances. This paragraph also gives us a glimpse of the early Christians at worship.

According to the description offered (v. 26), any member of the church might be expected to take part in the service. This does not mean everyone did, but each one could. Generally the Corinthians were energetic in their involvement. But this exuberance also created a problem in that everyone tried to speak at the same time. The result was disorder and confusion. Each one had something to add. One had a psalm. This has come to mean one of the 150 in the Old Testament Book of Psalms, but the word also denotes a song with instrumental accompaniment. In other words, someone presented a song before the congregation.[190] One had a "doctrine," which involves lessons and teaching in Christian truth. "A tongue" has already been discussed. One had "a revelation," which probably refers to some specific matter God had revealed to a believer, and it may involve prophecy. "An interpretation" refers to the interpretation of a message in tongues for the understanding and edification of all assembled. This is all fine as long as the foundational rule for these actions is applied: The gifts must first be of a kind to edify; then they must be used in an edifying manner.

Having set the standard for procedure in exercising the gifts of the Spirit, Paul now specifically shows the procedure regarding the exercise of "a tongue" (v. 27). Paul views the situation in the assembly where a man could speak aloud in an unknown tongue. The order is to be "by two, or at the most by three." This has generally been considered the number of times this particular manifestation should be exercised during one service. However, some view this as speaking at one particular time. There could be an interval of time and then another such sequence in the same service. The latter seems doubtful. "And that by course" refers to "in turn" (ASV). It involves an equal sharing of place and time with another. It appears that some had tried to speak at the same time as another. The result had been disorder. Paul is strongly opposed to such action.

"Let one interpret." There must be an interpretation, for the congregation must be edified (note v. 28). The presentation is to be clear, orderly, and spiritual. There seems no reason to stress this to mean only one person should interpret for the two or three speakers in tongues. What Paul indicates is prompt interpretation. As one person at a time speaks with a tongue, so one should then interpret. This interpreter may be the speaker in a tongue himself, or another used in the gift.

But if there is no interpreter present in the assembly, Paul specifies what the speaker in a tongue is to do (v. 28). He must refrain from public utterance and be content to speak in tongues in solitude unto God. The reason is that such public unintelligible utterance will not edify the congregation. This does not suggest that silence in privacy is best. He can then speak to benefit himself. This verse contradicts those who suggest that the operation of the gifts of the Spirit (here particularly the gift of tongues) is the result of an uncontrollable impulse and that the speaker becomes as a robot. The Spirit works through the will and personality of the individual.

Paul also shows that this order affects all the gifts of the Spirit, and is universal (v. 29). Prophecy, which Paul so highly recommended, is subject to the same standard and procedure as tongues. Everything must edify the congregation. Again we see the order of two or three at a service. "The other" is plural in the Greek. The utterance is not to be accorded uncritical acceptance. It is, rather, to be "judged" or discerned. The gift of discerning of spirits (12:10) could be in use here. We are also reminded of the instruction of 12:3 and 1 John 4:1-3. There is a necessary combination of prophecy and discerning. The listener must acknowledge the source of the utterance and then react accordingly. This verse also bears the thought that Paul did not wish to list one gift above another, except in terms of situation.

In this area, there must be a spirit of love and a desire to edify the congregation, and it must be demonstrated by a willingness to yield to another with a prophecy, so there will be no confusion or argument (v. 30). Perhaps two stand at the same time or "together" to give an utterance. The first, seeing this, should give way to the other. Or perhaps one is concluding an utterance and

129

another rises to speak. The speaker should give way to the other. It is within the prophet's power to do this, and to cease or keep silent for the good of another. In wisdom, according to the Holy Word, the individual should examine the circumstance and choose a course of edification. (See also v. 32.)

Paul is not "quenching the Spirit," but establishing an orderly, loving, edifying exercise of prophecy (v. 31). As each is moved on by the Spirit, in wisdom he will have the opportunity to exercise the gift. He will not be slighted, but will minister within the framework of order and "preferring one another." It is necessary that there be this order (vv. 29, 30), but the manifestations of the Spirit are also necessary. Therefore, all should prophesy one by one. Some have stated that this means all the congregation; others prefer only all the prophets. But anyone "filled with the Spirit" has the potential and opportunity of being used in one of these gifts of the Spirit. The manifestations of the Spirit are for the church. Even so, with due order and self-suppression each would have an opportunity to minister. In this way the church would enjoy the fullness of the powers of the Spirit given all its members.

The purpose is set forth: that "all may learn, and all may be comforted." There is an emphasis here on the thrice-repeated "all." If there is equal opportunity for utterance, then all the hearers will benefit. "All may learn" indicates part of the effect on the listener. He will be taught; he will be blessed and benefited. And the speaker will learn also; learn concerning the how, when, and where of prophecy. Of course, he will also be benefited spiritually by his own utterance. "All may be comforted" includes not only comfort, but also teaching and strength, exhortation and edification.

Paul explains how the order of verses 29-31 is possible (v. 32). He intimated at it while speaking concerning the order for tongues (v. 28). With this gift he speaks more plainly. The speaker is in control of himself. The "spirits of the prophets are subject to the prophets." This adds a subjective reason for regulation to the objective reason of verse 31. The speaker's will is important. The gift may be exercised in wisdom and love to accomplish the best possible ends. The false prophet, however, refuses to be subject to the rules of the Spirit and the Word of God. A prophet may desire to speak and have something important to say. Yet if there be good reason, it is within his power to remain silent.

For God is the God of peace (v. 33). The subjection in verses 30-32 is founded on a virtue and desire of God himself. He is a God of peace, which is naturally contrary to confusion, strife, and disorder. There is within the character of God a guarantee against disorderliness. And He has passed that on to the Church. When God brought this universe, and man, into being He established order and peace. The very laws of nature show a marked lack of confusion. It is foolish to suppose God's spiritual laws and works would be different. There is always order, peace, and edification in God's plans and purposes. What Paul in effect does is infer "order" by indicating God's underlying motive—peace. Ultimately then, Paul's directives on order in the assembly (and here especially applied to utterance) are based on the character and motives of God. God is a God of order and peace.

J. The Excellence of Propriety Among Women in the Public Assembly (14:33-36)

At this point a special note must be added on 14:33. There has been a difference of opinion on whether "as in all churches of the saints" should go with verse 33 or 34. Those who accept the former have several arguments: (1) Most of the ancients, Luther, and our versions connect it with verse 33, while most of the modern exegetes connect it with verse 34; (2) It is used as a support of the peace God confers that it is so in all the other churches; (3) To link it with verse 34 makes it come in clumsily before the mood of verse 34 and the repetition of "in the churches" is awkward.[191] This would then make these matters discussed of universal interest.

But those who connect this phrase with verse 34, seem to have the stronger case. The thought of verse 33 is complete in itself and needs no further qualification. Why should Paul wish to point to all the other churches? If any other church tolerated confusion it was also out of harmony with God. But how fitting is the reference to the practice of the other churches in reference to women's silence in the church. To associate it with verses 26-33, is to see the subject climax only to descend afterwards. To place it with verse 34 is to see it add strength to the subject under discussion.

To better understand this paragraph we must remember the background and custom in the churches; a custom that even today exists in the oriental world. The women sat on one side of the church and the men on the other. If a woman had a question, she had to call across the aisle to her husband, father, or another man. Furthermore, the women at Corinth had apparently taken their liberty and were causing distractions and confusion in the church assembly; or at the least the problem was fermenting and ready to appear. The result would be disastrous. Thus, Paul speaks to it.

Paul calls on this church to conform to the Christian practice in the churches (v. 34). He directs the women to keep silence in the church. How far does this go? Some have indicated that this means a woman is not to speak at all in the assembly, not even to prophesy. Those who defend this, point to the context of the chapter and to the fact that "obedience, as also saith the law" does not fit with just speaking in the assembly and not giving an address also. "Speaking in tongues" implies that "to speak" means more than to simply express oneself. Consequently, the idea is that Paul uses the general expression "to speak" to forbid all speaking in the services by women.[192]

However, this does not seem to argue well on the whole of Scripture, including 11:5. Morgan writes:

> Evidently there were women in Corinth given to careless and contentious talk, and that is what Paul was prohibiting. Certainly he was not saying that a woman had no right to pray or prophesy in the Church, because he had already given instructions as to how, and under what conditions, she was to do it. No, something else had crept into that fellowship meeting, the attitude taken by the women who were indulging in contentious, strident speech. Such were to keep silence there, and to remit the questions and discussions to the quietness and fellowship of the home.[193]

Moffatt asserts that Paul "never vetoed a devout woman from exercising, even at public worship, the prophetic gift which so many women in the primitive Church enjoyed." He believes the prohibition refers to their taking part in the discussion or interpretation of what was said by some prophet or teacher during the service.[194] And again we must remember Paul does say "to speak." Women most certainly were not to ask questions in the assembly (see v. 35). First Timothy 2:11-14, sheds some light on this passage. From this we may suggest that Paul is referring to speaking in the way of authoritative teaching and direction in the church.

"To be under obedience" is present tense and implies a lasting condition. Paul's omission of obedience "to the husbands" in this verse serves to note the general, dependent position of women. Paul rests on the authority of "the law" for this command regarding women. He probably has Genesis 3:16 in mind. This command cannot be cast aside as temporary for as we gather from this passage and chapter 11, Paul speaks of subjection which is part of the nature of the sexes and stems from God's work at creation. But we must be careful and correct in applying this to our present situation. And we must remember also what true Christian subjection is.[195]

But what if the motive for the woman's speaking were a true desire to learn something or have a question answered? What then? Paul bids the women (v. 35) not to take advantage, but to wait and ask their husbands at home the questions they have. In this Paul lays down a general rule. There are potential exceptions; but, in general, action contrary to these rules is shameful and against the nature of things and the Word of God (v. 34). It is not edifying. Whether Paul was correcting an abuse or a potential abuse we have no way of knowing for certain.

Paul reproves the situation strongly with the use of irony and questions to which he expects a negative answer (v. 36). By this he reminds his readers that they did not originate the Word, nor were they the only ones to receive it. Therefore, they had to conform to the Biblical pattern and Christian custom. Again selfishness and pride are rebuked. By these questions Paul suggests to the haughty Corinthians that they are desiring to take the place of God and are thinking they know better than God and His Word by trying to make His Word mean what they think it should. In regard to this directive on the utterance of women in the public assembly, or any other inspired directive, this could not be so.

133

K. The Summation on Utterance (and Edification and Spirituals) (14:37-40)

All that remains now is for Paul to fix his seal of authority to what has been written. While in the context this summation belongs particularly to the words of chapter 14, in a wider sense it probably belongs to the whole of Paul's discussion on public worship. Paul asserts his apostolic position and authority and his own reception of truth, and then once again reaffirms the directive to orderly manifestations and the overall theme of edification.

Paul makes claim to the fact that what he has written are the "commandments of the Lord." This gives us insight into how the New Testament writers viewed their inspiration, for no greater claim could be made. If a man thinks himself to be spiritual he will acknowledge the inspired truth of what is said here (v. 37). Paul makes no personal judgments. He leaves the answer as to possession of gifts, etc., to the individual. Whatever the case, he is to obey these commands from the Lord. And his reception of Paul's words will prove and decide the nature and condition of his prophecy or spirituality. Note John 8:47 in connection with Paul's following of Christ's pattern. There are those who conclude that "spiritual" must refer to "tongues," because Paul first mentions prophet and because of the context. But the word is more general than that and refers to one who has a spiritual gift and is able to judge what Paul says. Besides, elsewhere when Paul means a speaker in tongues, that is what he writes.

Verse 38 has been variously interpreted. One view states that if a man does not recognize as inspired truth what Paul has written, then Paul is finished with him. Let him remain ignorant. This view has some strong support. But some good manuscripts have a slightly different word[196] that is translated "he is not known," which could mean by the church, by God, or by the apostle, or by all of these. This is most reasonable. But if the verb is future, then the reference would be to the day of judgment. Whichever view is accepted, the fact remains that to refuse Paul's directives carries disastrous consequences. And these are dependent on the man's apprehension and pronouncement on the truth of Paul's words (from the Lord).[197]

"Wherefore" (v. 39) draws us to a conclusion. Paul wants his beloved brethren to seek spiritual manifestations. The tone of the chapter is reemphasized with the mention of prophecy and "tongues"; the tongue needing interpretation.

But at the same time, Paul reminds his readers these manifestations are to remain within the framework of edification and order (v. 40). Good taste and proper procedure are the rule of the day. Thus with brotherly love and masterly brevity Paul concludes his discussion on public worship and spiritual manifestations.

VII

The
Resurrection

(15:1-58)

A. The Message of Christ's Resurrection (15:1-11)

On the facts and principle established in this section rests the entirety of the gospel message. If it had been or were possible to disprove the resurrection of Jesus Christ, then Christianity must fold and silence its voice forever. But as is shown in this chapter, this message of life cannot be disproven. It rests on indisputable grounds. It can truly be called the rock on which our hope is based. This chapter sets forth this great central truth of the gospel more elucidatively than any other specific passage in the entire Bible. It not only declares the fundamental message, but also the dead end in denying the Resurrection and the clear promise in affirming it. In that sense, this chapter may be the greatest in the Word of God.

Paul begins with a gentle rebuke (vv. 1, 2). Rather than reminding them of the gospel he had preached, he declares it to them here. Some did not seem to realize the importance of what it meant, but they had received it. And they "stand" in it; "by which" or through which they "are saved." Clearly it is fundamental. The gospel is the means used to bring salvation. It is the sword of the Spirit. "Ye are saved" is present continuous, indicating continuous activity; "You are being saved." There is both a permanent, once-for-all, and a progressive sense. Salvation is a growing, deepening, inexhaustible experience.

"Keep in memory" ("if ye hold fast," *ASV*) has been differently interpreted. The word order is "by what word I preached to you if you hold fast." This may be considered a conditional clause with the "if" coming late to give emphasis to what precedes. It is not impossible in Greek construction. But this would seem to suggest

137

that Paul is demanding that they hold fast not only to the gospel but also to the actual words in which he presented it. This interpretation also requires a harsh grammatical inversion.

Another way of understanding the passage is to connect "by what word I preached the gospel to you" with "I make known" *(ASV)* at the beginning of verse 1, giving the sense: "I make known to you . . . in what terms I preached the gospel to you." Again the difficulty is "if you hold fast." Paul is not telling them something "if they hold it fast." He is declaring it whatever their attitude. But "if you hold fast" may be in parentheses or attached to "you are being saved."

"Unless ye have believed in vain" may refer to belief on an inadequate basis. If men are not really trusting Christ, their belief is empty. "Vain" includes the idea of at random, or without serious apprehension. Paul may also be making an early reference to what he refutes in verses 12-19.

Paul, being the faithful steward that he was, delivered to the Corinthians the very essence and substance, the core, of the gospel (vv. 3, 4). And this he did "first of all." Delivering this message was of singular rank and importance on Paul's list of things to accomplish. He delivered this message. It was a burden and a fire burning within. "Necessity" lay heavily upon him.

Paul delivered that which he had received. Whether he received it by direct revelation, as is mentioned in Galatians 1:12, or by other contributory channels we do not know. But three basic facts he did preach: (1) Christ's death for our sins; (2) Christ's burial; and (3) Christ's resurrection. The second of these facts links the others together, for it signalizes the completeness of His death and the reality of His resurrection. The death and burial of Christ are presented in the aorist tense as historical events; the Resurrection is emphatically placed in the perfect tense, as an abiding power. The perfect is used in this way six more times in this chapter,[198] but only twice in all the rest of the New Testament. And Christ's death, burial, and resurrection were accomplished to expiate for man's sin.[199] The Resurrection occurred on the third day. This specifically fulfilled the prophecies of Holy Writ. And this showed that in this case restoration to life ensued, when under normal circumstances the decaying of the corpse would have begun.

138

Further, there were witnesses to this great event (vv. 5-10). Jesus appeared to Peter. This manifestation by the Lord to Peter came before that given to the body of the apostles (Luke 24:34). It was not a vision; He could be seen by human eyes; the appearances were real. Peter was one of the leading apostles and his witness had a profound effect first on the other apostles and then on the church world as a whole. "The appearance to Peter is so important because he was one of the apostles, their leader we may say; because he was the first apostle to see the Lord; and because he saw the risen Lord on the very day of His resurrection."[200]

Jesus also appeared to "the twelve" (v. 5). This refers to the college of the apostles without exact regard to number. It was a designation for this group of men. Judas Iscariot was absent, and on the first meeting so was Thomas.

After that he was seen of "above five hundred brethren" (v. 6). The word used for "at once" is not so translated elsewhere and it is perhaps better translated "once for all," indicating that this was the culminating manifestation of the risen Christ, made at the general gathering of His brethren.[201] Paul notes that the majority of the group of over 500 remained alive at the writing of this Epistle. Perhaps due to the general youth of Christ's followers, only a few had "fallen asleep" or died. There was a continuing witness to the Resurrection. This is indeed the effect of the Resurrection, that death is converted into sleep in Christ. This may also have reference to Matthew 28:16.

Jesus also appeared to James (v. 7). The more fitting conclusion is that Paul is referring to James, the brother of the Lord.[202] This appearance, only mentioned here, explains the presence of "His brothers" among the 120 at Jerusalem and James' subsequent leadership of the Jerusalem church. At the time of this Epistle's writing, he held this high position and would have been an impressive witness.

Then Jesus appeared to "all the apostles" (v. 7). Interpretation here depends on whether we use the stricter or looser sense of "apostles." Paul, presumably aware of the absence of Thomas on the occasion of verse 5 and his consequent skepticism, may have written of this appearance to show that all the apostles saw Christ, and the resultant witness was complete and unqualified.

Lastly Jesus appeared to Paul (vv. 8-10). Paul describes himself as an untimely child, almost like an abortion, in the matter. Some find in this an indication of the suddenness and violence of Paul's birth into Christ; some see in it the unripe birth of one changed at a stroke from persecutor to apostle instead of maturing normally for his work.[203] It may well be this was one of the insults the Judaists threw at Paul. Perhaps his opponents took note of his personal appearance and his doctrine of free grace, and called him an abortion. Paul adopts the title and gives it a far deeper meaning.

"Of me also" lends emphasis to the matter. Even to Paul, the untimely child, Christ deigned to appear in resurrection power. A real sense of unworthiness hangs heavy in the air. He felt himself the "least of the apostles." The emphatic personal pronoun *I* quickly proves the great grace and condescension of Christ. Paul holds staunchly to two points: one is the high dignity of his position as an apostle; the other is his profound sense of unworthiness in the matter. He felt himself unworthy because he had persecuted the church of God. There is present a remorse that never left the apostle.[204] He had been active in the greatest of injustices; he had willfully persecuted the church of God. But the grace of God worked a marvelous transformation in his life. "I am what I am" by the grace of God. Paul was a sinner saved by grace; forgiven because of grace; a sinner redeemed and justified by the blood of Christ; a son of God; a joint-heir with Christ; an apostle and a servant of the Lord Jesus Christ. And this abundant grace brought with it abundant labor as well.

If at the outset Paul appeared last and least and unworthy of being an apostle, in execution he took the premier position. By his efforts he extended the kingdom of Christ over a larger area than the rest. Some say Paul does not actually say he has accomplished more but that he has worked harder. But he has to have some of the fruits in sight or grace would not be so greatly magnified, for grace is to be praised—"not I," but grace. Grace did the work; Paul was its instrument. Notice its continual accompaniment of Paul. The grace of God is pictured almost as a fellow laborer.

Paul concludes his comparison of himself and the other apostles and sums up his statement regarding the fact and evidence of Christ's resurrection (v. 11). Whether it was Paul or another (Peter, the Twelve, James, or one of the other witnesses listed), "we preach" and "ye believed." On the crucial matters of verses 1-4, and on the matter of the resurrection of Jesus Christ, whether it was Paul or Peter—Jerusalem or Corinth—there was not the slightest variation. The authoritative witness was unified and in one accord; they preached the same message—Jesus Christ raised from the dead. "So we preach" is present continuous, indicating practice. Thus, the foundation (Christ's resurrection) has been built for all that will follow on the resurrection of the body.

B. Consequences of Denying the Resurrection (of the Dead) (15:12-19)

Paul has asserted the fact of Christ's resurrection with barely a clue as to what his purpose in so writing is. Now he hits quickly and strongly. If the resurrection of Christ is true, how can anyone say the resurrection of the dead is not also a fact? The two are tightly linked. It is obvious that some at Corinth had doubted the resurrection of the dead. Such skepticism wrecked the faith of the church, just as party divisions destroyed its love. Paul puts forth his full strength to grapple with this difficulty. Apparently these did not, however, doubt the personal resurrection of Jesus Christ. But they would not admit the recovery of the body. Perhaps Christ's resurrection was viewed as a unique, symbolic occurrence bringing about a wholly spiritual deliverance; a literal, full release from the flesh and matter.

This argument had its parallels in history with such as the doctrine of the Sadducees (Acts 23:8), and countless illustrations from the superstitions of the Greeks. Some Greek philosophies theorized that the soul continued to exist, but the body died forever. Here "some" claimed the idea, not many. Their idea belonged to the "wisdom of this age."

It must be pointed out that from the beginning of his refutation, Paul asserts the impossibility of this error ("how say some") and concludes that the erring Christians are doing violence to the Christian belief. Paul's opposing argument will follow two basic lines: If the Resurrection is untrue, then the Christian faith and its witnesses are false; and if this resurrection is not real, then neither are the effects derived from it.

141

Paul begins then with the idea that the resurrection of Jesus Christ is logically impossible if there is a denial of bodily resurrection (v. 13). Christ's resurrection was not even an exception; it was a pattern for many who would follow. If there is no resurrection of dead ones (dead bodies), neither has Christ been raised because His body was dead and then raised to life by God. Therefore, the assumption by these Corinthians is wrong. A universal negative cannot be accepted if one fact to the contrary exists.

If the fact is untrue, then the testimony, of necessity, is untrue and hollow. If the message is hollow, building on an untrue fact, then the faith is also hollow, building on an untrue message and fact. The gospel becomes empty; it is robbed of all its vitality. Step by step Paul tears down their doctrinal error. Even here the Corinthians must agree with Paul, for they know of their own faith; they had believed and accepted the apostles' preaching.

The additional consequence would be, if the dead are not raised, that Paul and his fellow witnesses would be found to have given lying testimony of the worst kind—about God (v. 15). They had testified that God had raised up Jesus. Paul always imputes the raising of Jesus to God who, thereby, gave His verdict on the matter.[205] Thus, they would be literally testifying against God. Either Christ arose from the dead or the apostles had lied in affirming it; there is no other solution. The second possibility never even enters Paul's mind. Such a falsehood would have wronged God.

Verse 16 acts like a hinge for this section. What has already been said is repeated with a minor adjustment. Paul has discussed the falsity of faith and witness if there is no raising of the dead. Now he will discuss the unreality of effect if this fact is not true. The intention is to carry this argument to its end and prove its utter absurdity.

The effects of denying the resurrection of Jesus Christ are listed, one of which is that faith is ineffective because it is built on a false foundation; therefore, our sin has not been removed and we are still sinners (v. 17). A faith is useless which does not save from sin. But without Christ's resurrection, both our justification and sanctification are absent. But this is in disagreement with experience; these readers had experienced salvation. Paul and the apostles were valid witnesses. Christ had been raised from the dead.

Paul moves through the dark maze to further miserable conclusions necessitated if Christ has not been raised from the dead (v. 18). He speaks of those who have "fallen asleep in Christ." The sense of His presence and the promises of the Word have turned death into sleep. But if the Resurrection is denied, then they have really perished. They have died "yet in [their] sins," and thus in ruin and damnation. Laying down to "rest" untroubled, they would find cruel deception. In such a case there would be no hope beyond the grave. This would make Christianity no better than Greek paganism which thought death to be the adversary that in the end defeated all men. But as Paul writes elsewhere, Christ has removed the sting of death (15:55), and he can speak of death as "gain" (Philippians 1:21). But again, only if there is a resurrection.

The bitterness of the last step in this argument shows itself (v. 19). It is almost with a sigh of relief that we realize Paul has come to the end of this negative aspect. Yet the very blackness and falsity of this denial of the Resurrection is a sign of the light Paul has implied throughout and will show forth brightly in the next paragraph. If hope in Christ exists in this world and life only, then there is no present deliverance from sin and no future inheritance in heaven, and we are of all men most to be pitied. For an empty, fruitless hope without foundation, by a hollow ineffectual faith, Christians have made great sacrifices then, even giving their lives for the gospel. No wonder the Christian would be the object of great pity.

Paul has effectively combated the error of denying the resurrection of the body. He has done so by pointing out the black consequences of such a position. Now he cannot remain on the dismal side, for he is prepared to break forth in the song of glorious assurance regarding Christ's resurrection and the resurrection of the dead.

C. The Assurance of Christ's Resurrection (15:20-28)

"But now" (v. 20) Paul unconditionally asserts the resurrection of Christ. All the ugly consequences of verses 12-19 are untrue because there is a resurrection of the dead, and Christ has been raised. Paul uses the perfect tense of the verb *to rise*. Not only did

Christ rise, He also continues permanently as the risen Lord.[206] Christ's resurrection makes resurrection for the members of His body inevitable. Christ is the firstfruits of many "brothers" who shall follow. They lie asleep (their bodies, that is) in Christ and shall respond in that great day to His call to rise. There is an allusion to the first harvest sheaf of the Passover, which was presented in the sanctuary on the 16th Nisan (possibly the day of Christ's resurrection). The first ripe sheaf was an earnest of the harvest and was consecrated to God and given to Him in acknowledgment of what He had done and in anticipation of what would follow.[207] Christ was not the first to rise from the dead. Indeed, He had raised some himself. But they died again. His resurrection was to a life that knows no death. His is the life and fact that conquered death. The resurrection, then, has really begun.

Christ is identified with those sleeping in death because He is the antitype of Adam; the Medium of life as Adam was of death. Adam represented carnality, sin, and death; Christ represents spirituality, holiness, and life (vv. 21, 22). When man sinned he passed into a new state, one controlled and symbolized by death itself. But Christ brought life. If death had not come through a man there would have been no need for Christ to take on the form of a man and die as a man to redeem the human race. Christ then is the principle and root, the Source, of resurrection life. There is also the suggestion that, contrary to some, death is not a law or necessity of fate. Man brought it on himself by an event in history; and it is removable, in degree, by another event in history—Calvary and the Resurrection.

Adam is pictured as the natural, earthly founder of humanity of which Christ is the spiritual, heavenly counterpart and the giver of new life. Some have concluded that Paul says in verse 22 that "all" (especially the second "all") men shall be made alive in Christ, even the sinful dead, and that Paul is referring to the resurrection of all the dead. But this is difficult to support in view of the context. Paul is linking the risen Christ with the Christian dead, as yet unresurrected. This view would also place grammatical stress on the wrong point. The idea is that as death in every case is grounded in Adam, so life in all cases is grounded in Christ. All will not rise in Christ, as certainly as they die in Adam.

But while there is a unity in nature and principle, there is a difference in agreement and a distinction in order (v. 23). Christ was raised as the firstfruit, then at His coming His people shall be raised. The thought is of a military division. There is the Captain, above all in His solitary glory; and there is His army, now sleeping, which shall rise at His trumpet's sound, at the call of the bugle. (See also 1 Thessalonians 4:16.) Truly, "the King is coming!"

Christ's second advent, of which the Rapture is a part, concludes this history of the world (v. 24). "Then [is] the end," which indicates the end of the drama of sin and redemption in which "the Adam" and "the Christ" have played their respective parts. "Then" indicates taking place at an unspecified time afterward. The end shall be culminated by Christ's delivering the kingdom to God the Father before which He shall have abolished all opposition, "all rule, and all authority and power." The two verbs indicate distinct but related actions. When every opposing force has been destroyed, then Christ shall lay His kingdom at the Father's feet.

"To God, even the Father" or "to Him who is God and Father" explains the reason for Christ's action of submission. The thought is not one of loss, but of giving to another what was designed for Him. It is Christ's aim to please the Father at all times, and while this was historically accomplished at the cross, it shall be done finally when Christ is able to present a kingdom governed by His will and filled with obedient sons. This does not indicate a demotion of Christ; it is not the cessation of Christ's dominion, but the inauguration of Christ's eternal kingdom; it is not the termination of Christ's rule but of the reign of sin and death. "All" is complete.

Verse 25 adds to the thought. Paul is thinking of the culmination of Christ's kingship. There is a compelling necessity about Paul's "must." God has decided finally on this matter and no uncertainty is involved. There is a reference here to Psalm 110:1, which indicates the Messiah's obligation and power. Paul inserts this section of general eschatology to indicate Christ's kingship which points to the task He fulfills today as the risen Lord. The work Christ is doing now is the prelude to and the notice of the absolute end.

Paul has spoken of the event occurring at the "end" of earthly history and of the event preceding that, which is the subjection of all rule and power to that of Christ. The last enemy to be totally brought to nothing is death (v. 26). This stands in opposition to the position held by "some" in verse 12. These say there is no resurrection; Paul counters that there is to be no death. Death shall be robbed of all its control and power. It shall be abolished. This is really a climax in Paul's argument. As one writer points out, this false belief has been confuted in fact by Christ's resurrection; in experience by the work of grace in believers; and now in principle by its contrariety to the purpose and plan of redemption which means the "death of Death."[208]

Verse 27 is like a supplement to Paul's main thought in verses 20-26, but it reaffirms the unlimited dominion of Christ and the fact that only through His absolute victory can the kingdom of God be consummated. There is a reference to Psalm 8, which promised to man complete rule over his domain. As man, Christ stands forth as Deliverer and Conqueror for man, for He has conquered death. "All things are subdued" is the announcement of the Son. With the abolition of death, His commission is ended and the travail of His soul is satisfied. The first part of verse 28 reaffirms objectively, as a matter of fact, what was issued subjectively as the verdict by Christ himself on His own finished work. "But" (v. 27, *ASV*) adds a self-evident assertion concerning God the Father. There is behind the messianic reign the absolute supremacy of God.

And when this subjection of "all things" to Christ has been completed, then Christ shall be subjected to God the Father (v. 28). This simply involves the subjection of sonship. There is no inferiority of nature or removal of power, but the free submission of love. This was the spirit that motivated Christ in His earthly ministry. His intention was always to glorify the Father, who in turn glorified the Son. And the purpose of all this is fixed in conclusion: that God be "all in all"; that God's will be everywhere observed and His being everywhere immanent.

D. The Application of Belief
(in the Bodily Resurrection) (15:29-34)

"Baptized for the dead" (v. 29) has been debated for many

centuries. It is one of the most difficult Scripture passages to come to a decision on in the Bible. However, the major theories must be discussed.

The Marcionites once believed as the Mormons do now that the apostle Paul clearly approved such a ceremony. The Latin writers repeated Ambrosiaster and taught that Paul indicated some Corinthians who, out of good faith, were baptized for their friends who had died unbaptized. The Greek fathers followed Tertullian's and Chrysostom's view that this was the baptism received for the resurrection of our dying, mortal bodies. Luther felt Paul's text referred to baptism administered on the sepulchers of martyrs. Calvin explained it as baptism of dying people, and Theodore Beza saw it as the washing of the dead.[209] Thus the controversy has continued throughout the history of the Church. Certain of the current views do seem impossible however.

There are those, of which the Mormons form a part, that believe this was a vicarious baptism in which living friends were baptized for those who died unbaptized. There are examples of this in earlier history and even before the Christian era in Jewish history. Chrysostom explained it. They had a living man hidden under the bed of the deceased. When they spoke to the dead one, the living replied and was baptized for the dead. J. Reuben Clark wrote: "Hundreds of thousands of those who have gone to the other side have been blessed by the performance of this vicarious ordinance in their behalf."[210]

It seems utterly ridiculous that anyone could interpret this as the meaning here. Paul's alluding to the custom does not indicate he approved of it; rather, the opposite is implied. Ellicott indicates that Paul differentiated himself from those who believed it by using the word *they*. He further writes: "It is no proof to others; it is simply the *argumentum ad hominem*." He also indicates that Paul was apparently asking a question concerning the reaction of those who were baptized substitutes for the dead.[211] Both of these views seem unlikely. It is difficult to suppose that the living could be baptized for the dead; for baptism does not always appear necessary for salvation. Vicarious baptism, if advocated here, would do away with Paul's views. But at the same time, there are those who say Paul could not have even been alluding to it because using superstition would have opened him to even more severe reproof.[212]

Some understand it to mean baptizing over the dead, which is said to have been an early custom that testified of the hope of the resurrection. It does not, however, appear that any such doctrine was in practice in the apostles' time.

Others understand it of those who were baptized for the sake of the martyrs because of the constancy of their religion. Some probably became Christians by observing this too. But the church at Corinth apparently had not seen a lot of persecution at this time nor had many converts been made by the constancy of the martyrs.

Henry's explanation that these may have meant some Corinthians who were taken by the hand of God may come closer to the truth. First Corinthians 11:30 states that many were sick or dead (because of disorderly conduct at the Lord's table). Some might have been frightened into believing, and persons baptized on such an occasion might be said to have been baptized on their account or for the dead. His implication is that these had done right and acted wisely, which would have been untrue if the dead did not rise, for they might provoke God and hasten their death.[213]

Neither can we overlook those who say that the bond and tie between the dead and the living is the resurrection and the future of blessedness.[214]

But perhaps the most logical explanation is offered by those who accept the view that the Christians and especially the apostles foresaw that their faith would cost them the loss of all things, including perhaps life; thus, in proceeding to baptism they went to their virtual death (and perhaps teamed it with the hope of future blessedness and friendships, etc.).[215] Adam Clarke describes it:

If there be no resurrection of the dead, those who, in becoming Christians expose themselves to all manner of privations, crosses, severe sufferings, and a violent death, can have no compensation, nor any motive sufficient to induce them to expose themselves to such miseries. But as they receive baptism as an emblem of death in voluntarily going under the water, so they receive it as an emblem of the resurrection unto eternal life, in coming up out of the water; thus they are baptized for the dead in perfect faith of the resurrection.[216]

Scripture refers much to the peril of the apostles and other missionaries.[217] These faced hourly hazards with the hope of future "joy" and security because of the resurrection of the dead. If the resurrection of the dead is not a fact, this constant exposure to danger is foolhardy, even madness (v. 30).

Paul writes of his "daily dying" and his affliction in Asia (2 Corinthians 1:8-11; this may have been in Ephesus). He had not been in this situation at Corinth (Acts 18:8ff.), and lest they think he was exaggerating, he makes his exclamation "that glorying . . . Lord" (v. 31, *ASV*). His glorying, however, is held in Christ Jesus. "Daily I die" comes first in the Greek for emphasis. Paul's danger was both real and constant. Perhaps as well as daily facing danger, he in himself daily abandoned his life. Moffatt translates: "Not a day but I am at death's door! I swear it by my pride in you, brothers, through Christ Jesus our Lord" (v. 31). "Thus Paul boasts in the results of his apostolic work, which is exactly that for which he dies daily."[218]

Paul earned poverty, infamy, and pain; if there is no "day of Christ" when his "glory" shall be full, he has been a fool (v. 32). It is difficult to ascertain whether Paul actually fought in the Ephesian arena or not. Some older scholars conclude that he did. However, there are certain points that do not support this view: (1) Paul was a Roman citizen and Roman citizens could not ordinarily be compelled to fight in the arena; (2) No such experience is listed in the trials described in 2 Corinthians 11; (3) It appears from Acts 19:31-40 that Paul had friends among the ranking officials at Ephesus who probably would have prevented such a thing; and (4) Part of the city had attacked him and Paul probably had in mind those men in Ephesus who had fiercely opposed him and tried to take his life; thus, he applies this phrase metaphorically. The closeness of "I die daily" and "I fought with beasts" *(ASV)* supplies exegetical reason for regarding both verbs in somewhat of a figurative sense.

Morbid unbelief will produce a certain desperation and sensuality (v. 32). Paul quotes from Isaiah 22:13, which reveals the recklessness bred by the absence of a hope of life after death. This citation might have provided an axiom for the popular Epicureanism. It is also an excellent example of ancient popular morals and attitudes. Eating, drinking, then dying was the very best that could be had, they thought. However, this would only be true if there were no resurrection of the dead.

This disbelief in the resurrection was in keeping with the Corinthians' low ethics and heathen association. Paul charges them: "Be not deceived"; "Do not err" (Grosheide, *Commentary on First Corinthians*, p. 377); "Do not be misled" *(NIV)*. The Corinthians were attempting to be too broad in their spacious allowance of tenets of skepticism and demoralizing intent. The line the apostle quotes, "Evil . . . manners" (v. 33), is attributed to Menander (322 B.C.), of the New Comedy, an Epicurean. But this proverb was probably around long before Menander.[219]

Paul makes a startling call to awake and to sin not, to men fallen into a spiritual stupor under the seductions of sensualism, heathen society, and intellectual pride (v. 34). *Awake* originally had the sense of becoming sober after drunkenness. Paul urges them to sober righteousness. Robertson and Plummer suggest that the skeptics claimed to be sober thinkers and denied belief in the resurrection as wild enthusiasm. If so, Paul's verb really fits.[220]

Some among the Corinthians had no knowledge of God. This asserts a characteristic, persistent condition which these "some" shared with the heathen. Paul spoke this to move the Corinthians to shame. The error that had arisen was caused basically by a lack of real knowledge of God. For Paul to write as he did must have been humiliating for the Corinthians because they prided themselves on their knowledge, especially of God. Conduct and morals are also involved here. Paul is certainly discussing correct doctrine at this point. But doctrine affects living, and wrong doctrine will lead to sinful living. What gnaws at the root, damages the fruit! Paul connects wrong living with wrong thinking. Those who have faith in the resurrection will apply that faith in everyday living and, consequently, live in belief. Perhaps it is as C. S. Lewis wrote in *Mere Christianity* (New York: MacMillan Co., 1964): "Aim at heaven and you will get earth thrown in. Aim at earth and you get neither."

E. The Nature of the Resurrection Body—An Explanation (15:35-49)

Paul has established beyond question the fact of the resurrection. He now intends to answer those questions regarding the nature and experiential side of the resurrection of the body (v. 35). These questions were asked by either an honest, earnest inquirer or a skeptical objector. It is probable, in view of verse 36, "Thou fool," that the latter was meant. These questions refer to possibility and conceivability. Both are doubted in regard to the resurrection of the body. These questions claim the resurrection to be absurd, for what body could rise out of a corpse, suitable to the undying spirit. But each one is answered as we continue.

"Thou foolish one" (*ASV*, v. 36) quickly asserts Paul's estimate of the skeptical question. It was a foolish, even a stupid, question showing a lack of spiritual understanding and faith in God. Paul draws on an analogy from nature. He personally involves the objector. If this foolish man would only look at the fields, at his own work, he would realize that nature carries an analogy. The farmer plants a seed in the ground. But it cannot produce a plant or a crop and enlarge and enhance itself unless it first dies. But if it dies, then it is "quickened" and produces a much greater yield. Thus, life comes out of death. Notice that the seed does not give itself life; God gives it life. Paul does not explain the *modus operandi,* but what he does show is that the mystery creates no doubt or prejudice against the reality, for the same mystery is present in the vegetating seed. With this example from nature so close to us, why should anyone think the transformation of a dead body is impossible? While the form is changed, and the seed and sprout appear with differences, yet there is an essential identity that links what is sown and what sprouts together and assures us they are one and the same.

Paul answers the second question of verse 35 with the same analogy (v. 37). The purpose of the sower is to see and receive a different ("new") form or product from his seed. Yet the sower knows it is the "same" body or seed. The truth of this lower "resurrection" supports the conceivability of the higher resurrection. "It may chance . . . grain" refers to the fact that the grain of wheat gives to the physical senses no more promise of the future body than any other seed or grain. But the raised body shall be more wonderful than the body that was buried.

Paul concludes the sentence with a reference to the fact that this which arises from the dead seed is a God-given body. So also, we might add, is the resurrection body. God gives the body as He

151

"willed" (v. 38, *Confraternity*), not as He "wills," in accordance with His creational decree by which the continuation and propagation of earthly life was determined from the beginning.[221] The divine will is the joint between seed and plant.

The second half of verse 38 adds the fact that as God finds a fit body for each of the numberless planted seeds, so He will provide a fit body for man's redeemed, glorified nature. While in this small division this is the only place Paul so explicitly mentions the divine oversight, it nevertheless remains that this is central to Paul's entire discussion. The man sows; the seed dies; the plant raises by the power of God. It is an ordained rising; so shall it be with the resurrection of the body. Notice also God's continuous participation and involvement with this earth. God gives continually the proper body to each seed.

The remainder of this section (vv. 39-41) supports what Paul has just put forth. He speaks of the varied forms in nature and the appropriateness of each for the life it clothes (v. 39). He speaks particularly of animal life. In the zoological realm there is countless differentiation rather than uniformity. The corporeity of each division listed here—men, beasts, birds, fishes—has been established according to individual constitution and needs. And if God can find the precise body necessary for these lower forms, and even for mortal man, can He not also provide the proper body for the resurrected man?

Paul adds to his illustrations by referring to celestial and terrestrial bodies (v. 40). Again, countless differentiation is noted. There are both heavenly and earthly bodies. But what does Paul mean by "heavenly bodies" *(NIV)*? Some believe it refers to bodies for celestial inhabitants, such as the angels.[222] Paul returns in verses 47-49 to the same contrast in the antithesis between "the earthy man" and the "heavenly." Paul may well be thinking more of the risen Christ than of angels. Also the counterpart to "heavenly bodies," in our sense of the terms, would be "the earth," not "bodies terrestrial."[223]

Others believe that verse 41 in connection with verse 40 suggests the sun and moon, etc., as the "heavenly bodies" in Paul's mind. One interesting support of this view is that it is unlike Paul to speak of bodies, one class of which we cannot see or imagine (the bodies of angels), while making such a comparison. Rather, he would more likely write about that which could be easily seen and compared. A few combine the above interpretations by attributing to the apostle the view of Philo and others, that the stars are animated and to be identified with Old Testament "angels." But this is not Biblically possible.[224]

While the heavenly and earthly bodies are alike in the sense that they are both bodies, there is a vast difference in "glory" between the two. Paul specifically mentions the sun, moon, and stars as examples (his concluding ones) of the point of differentiation in body and "glory" (v. 41). Each has a glory distinctly its own, prepared by God. The sun, the moon, and each star has its unique function and place in God's creation and, therefore, each has its own glory, given it by God. All are glorious, but there are degrees.

The phrase "so also . . . of the dead" (v. 42) is really both a summary and a transitional sentence. Paul has written of examples from nature supporting the idea and nature of the resurrection body. Now he summarizes and makes a direct application to his theme, the resurrection body. From there he begins to describe its change more directly and specifically. Paul first lists the states of both natural and resurrection bodies and the changes involved. There will be a change from corruption to incorruption. *The Expositor's Greek Testament* makes an interesting comment regarding "sown." Many interpret this verb as figuring burial. But this would confuse the analogy. "Sowing" is distinct from "dying." It also would not coincide with the fact that a sick man is called weak, not a corpse (v. 43), and with "natural" in verse 44. (Also note verses 50-54.) Therefore, the conclusion is presented that our present life is the "seed time" (Galatians 6:7) and our "mortal bodies" (Romans 8:10ff.) are in the germinal state, which shall conclude with death and out of which a different "body" will spring.[225]

Sowing brings to mind certain antitheses of which corruption-incorruption is the first. Corruption refers most correctly to the perishableness of man's actual physique. The word refers primarily to the body's gradual decaying tendencies. The "incorruption" of the resurrection state is well placed here. The major objection of the Greeks to this thought was that the body is basically corruptible. This is because they thought only of the body of flesh and blood. Paul agrees that corruption is a property of the earthly body. But the resurrection body will be a transformed body of which incorruption is a characteristic.

A second change is noted, that of dishonor to glory (v. 43). There is nothing honorable about the body that is put into the grave, without rights, and left to decay. Its decomposition would in a short time cause us to shrink back in horror. But the Greeks' rising doubts on the dishonorable nature of the present body are not valid; it shall be changed into a glorious body. As the beautiful plant far surpasses the seed from which it sprang, so shall the resurrection body far surpass this present one in glory.

A third change is noted, that of weakness to power. Exercise and strengthen it as we might try (and the Greeks did), the body remains a weak instrument excelled by the mind in it and exceeded in power (for its size) by many in the animal kingdom. And at death it is totally powerless. But the resurrection body shall be transformed; it shall be raised by God in power!

Paul shows the distinctions in nature between the natural and the spiritual body (v. 44). Paul adds another "it is sown." But this time it involves a summation in effect of the other three changes, while at the same time adding an important point which Paul will enlarge. "Natural" has to do with the present life in all its aspects, especially as it stands in opposition to the supernatural life. Paul may not have in mind sinfulness; rather, this passage seems to say this present body is suited to this present life; it is adapted to its present functions. But it is not fitted for the "heavenly" life.

"Spiritual" refers, on the other hand, to the type of body needed for the world to come. Therefore, God will change the "natural" body to a "spiritual" body that will answer the needs of that future life. Here Paul inserts another point in the logic of the resurrection body: "If [should be added in the *KJV*] there . . . natural . . . also a spiritual body" (v. 44, *ASV*). From the fact of sense, Paul moves to the fact of faith. Both phases of existence remain solid facts. On the principle of verse 38, a spiritual body is necessary. Paul is asserting that the existence of the natural body (and no one could argue that fact) argues the existence of this spiritual body.

Paul further explains the different natures by mentioning those of Adam and Christ. It appears (v. 45) that Paul's point is that the basic characteristic of man from the beginning has been

154

the "soul." This first Adam passed on his nature to all who followed. As the father of the human race his nature is stamped on it. Paul adds that Christ, in comparison, "was made a quickening ['life-giving,' *ASV*] spirit." And He is the progenitor of the spiritual race. The whole of Scripture witnesses to this. And as such, He stamps His nature on those who are "in Him." But not only is this "last Adam" the pattern for all those in Him, but He is also the source of that life which shall result in the resurrection body. "Adam" is here repeated to maintain Christ's humanity and our bodily relationship to Him.

In "life-giving spirit" some see a reference to the Incarnation, the Resurrection, or the Second Advent. The best view on the basis of the context seems to be the reference to His resurrection. Not only did He at this time enter a "spiritual" and ultimate form, He also entered this state to pass it on to His followers.[226]

Paul reminds his readers, however, that there is a logical and necessary order: first natural, then spiritual. There is an affirmed development from lower to higher. First comes natural birth; then follows spiritual birth. But we must be reminded that while the necessary order is natural first, then spiritual, Paul is not equating the two; he is simply establishing the order, for the spiritual far outweighs the natural even in the context of the body. Paul is recording two historical facts. Perhaps his readers were tempted to consider this abstractly and conclude that the spiritual ought to precede the natural. The next step would be to argue that the spiritual, being the original, ought alone to remain. Thus, the conclusion would be a rejection of the bodily resurrection. Paul cuts short such thinking.

Paul ties in the origin of the two natures (v. 47). The first man had an earthly origin. While Paul has in mind specifically the idea of bodily origin, the words *of the earth, earthy,* denote the whole quality of this life. This first man necessarily refers to Adam, and reminds us of Genesis 2:7. "Earthy" is different from "earth" and means "made of dust." "The first man" was bound to this earth.

The "second man" refers to Jesus Christ.[227] "Man" is contrasted with "man." "First" and "second" suggest that these were men who had great significance for others, and the true humanity of both is set forth. But while Christ appeared on this earth (He "took upon him the form of . . . men" [Philippians 2:7] and lived, died, and rose again), His origin was not of this earth, but of heaven. Any real reference to the preexistent Christ here is doubtful. Paul is presenting a historical relationship between Adam and Christ. This could and probably would involve the Incarnation. But most specifically Paul is presenting Christ as following and displacing Adam in the course of human history. And He came from heaven to do it.

All of Adam's descendants are in Adam's image just as all of Christ's followers are in His image (v. 48). The question has been asked as to whether this is purely a physical distinction between pre- and post-resurrection states of the same men, or a moral implication is involved. It seems there is some moral connotation involved, in view of the context (especially v. 49) and other passages, such as Romans 6:4; Philippians 3:17-21; Colossians 3:1-4. The context is important. All men are patterned after Adam in that they have "earthy" bodies. But Christians enjoy another relationship also, that with Christ; and because of this, they are "heavenly." This most certainly involves the present implications mentioned above, but there is also that future additive which must not be excluded. In the words of 1 John 3:2: "We shall be like him. . . ."

Our view of verse 48 is important to the concept of verse 49. "We have borne" involves the idea of what is continual and habitual. "Image" is used of man being made in God's image. It may denote simply representation, as did the image of the emperor on coins, or it may be used more precisely. "Here it will be the image that corresponds to and reproduces the original."[228]

There are differing views as to how the phrase "we shall also bear" should read. One view accepts the larger (moral) scope of verse 48, and therefore accepts the hortatory "we shall also bear" (v. 49), and so reads this: "Let us wear also the image of the Heavenly One." The "image" would embrace the entire "man," not just the body. We are exhorted elsewhere to "put on Christ" (Romans 13:14; Galatians 3:27), with the idea that to wear His moral likeness here means also to wear His bodily likeness after the resurrection.[229] A majority of the more ancient manuscripts do read, "Let us bear."

Another view, however, urges: "We shall bear." Those who support this regard "let us bear" as a primitive corruption of the text by scribes attempting exhortation. It is viewed as a marked digression of Paul's usual approach. "Let us bear" makes it appear as though this "image" were something men could accomplish by their own efforts. The context is viewed as in favor of "we shall bear." And some good authorities do support this.

This paragraph began with the assertion of a spiritual or resurrection body and then described it. Paul ends it with the assurance that we shall be given this spiritual or resurrection body.

F. The Assured Conquest of the Resurrection (15:50-58)

The apostle now approaches the fitting conclusion for his argument. The key has rested in the supremacy of Jesus Christ. Now he also quiets the minds of the living and exhorts his readers to worthy accomplishment of their life's work in Christ because of the fact and hope of the resurrection.

Paul makes two assertions that parallel what he has just written (v. 50). The first is that "flesh and blood cannot inherit the kingdom of God." With "brethren" we see Paul's personal involvement and bond in this matter. "Flesh and blood" are used to denote first substance (flesh), then the life-giving principle (blood) of this physical body. There is an opposition between the physical body and the spiritual body. The "natural" body is unfit for the kingdom of God. It must be changed. "Inherit" points to the rights and possessions of believers, as yet unrealized. The second assertion, built on the first, is that corruption (perishableness) cannot inherit incorruption (imperishableness). There must be a necessary change.

Having said that, Paul replies to those who might have wondered if they had to die before they could be changed (v. 51). "Behold" calls emphatic attention to the declaration that follows. "Mystery" speaks of a secret that is totally impossible for man to penetrate. It points to the possibility of man's knowing, but it also points to a secret that God has chosen to make known to man. Men could never have discovered what will happen at the resurrection, but God has revealed it. "We" is in general usage and probably not intended to suggest that Paul was indicating Christ would come in his lifetime. He lived as though Christ might come at any time, but he did not know when Christ was coming, nor did

157

he ever claim to. Some will not die, but whether among that group or not, dead or alive, "we shall all be changed." "Sleep" again describes death, for "total" death is foreign to the Christian. The question here is just the opposite of that in 1 Thessalonians 4:13-18.

Paul uses three vivid phrases to describe this change that will take place (v. 52). "In a moment" is "that which cannot be cut or divided," the smallest possible. We get our word *atom* from it. It describes the instantaneousness of the event. "In the twinkling of an eye" reemphasizes the instantaneousness of the event. "Twinkling" suggests the idea of throwing. It refers to the time it takes to cast a glance or flutter an eyelid. "At the last trump" suggests the solemn finality of this transformation. There is evidence in the Old Testament, Gospels, and contemporary Judaism associating the trumpet with the events of the end time. The trumpet was often used in festivity and triumph.[230]

The facts are repeated. The trumpet shall sound. At Christ's return, as is mentioned elsewhere, a trumpet will sound. The Christian dead shall be raised incorruptible or imperishable in and by the resurrection. "We shall be changed" marks a distinction between the Christian dead and the Christian living, the latter of which is meant by this phrase. (For "we," see the note on verse 51.) The Christian living will not have to die first, nor will they be left behind; they will also be changed.

The necessity of change explained negatively in verse 50 is now reaffirmed positively as being due to our nature and relations (v. 53). "This" body of which Paul was painfully conscious, must of necessity put on incorruption and immortality. It is bound to do so. But the power to fulfill this obligation comes from God. "To put on" is the usual word for putting on clothing. This "change" is now represented as an investiture with incorruption and immortality.

It is characteristic of Paul to see fulfillment of Scripture in all of this (v. 54). "When" indicates time. When these things shall have taken place, then certain Old Testament prophecies will be fulfilled. "Corruptible" putting on "incorruption" and "mortal" putting on "immortality" are what must come to pass to fulfill the Old Testament. The quotation is from Isaiah 25:8, and there is a parallel with 1 Corinthians 15:24, 27. The destruction of this "last" enemy, this "king of terrors," indicates absolute victory for Christ and His followers. "Swallowed" presents a dramatic figure and expresses complete destruction. And not only is death destroyed so it can do no more harm, but also all of its apparent victories in days and years past are undone, reversed, destroyed. We shall live in absolute victory!

Paul can contain himself no longer. He breaks into a song of triumph over death (v. 55). It is in the strain of Hosea's anticipation of Israel's resurrection from national death. (See Hosea 13:14.) The words of Hosea are freely adapted. "Sting" gives us the picture of death as an insect with a deadly sting. The great harmfulness of death is pictured. But there is more than a question here. "Where" denotes an exclamation of victory, a challenge, that must be answered by, "Nowhere!" Death holds no permanent victory. We are victors over death and its sting.

Paul summarizes the doctrine of sin, law, and death (expounded more fully in Romans 4 to 8 and Galatians 3) and interprets the reference in verse 55 (v. 56). Sin gives death its power; it is its sting. It gives death its penal character, its humiliating form, and its "bondage of corruption." To those who fall "asleep" in Jesus Christ, however, the sting of death has been removed because Christ has taken the sense of guilt and fear of judgment. Sin in turn receives its power from the Law. We have here a six-word condensation of Paul's teaching of the relation between sin and the Law: The Law imposes on sinful man necessary but impossible requirements, promising salvation on fulfillment of impossible terms and death on nonfulfillment. This in effect "extends" sin and involves the sinner in hopeless guilt. When death is "the wages of sin" it has a deadly sting. When death, because of pardoned sin, ushers into the immediate presence of the Lord, it is gain, not loss.

Paul ends his song of triumph by asserting the Source of our victory (v. 57). The apostle finally links his doctrine of the bodily resurrection and transformation of the believer to his basic teaching on justification and forgiveness of sins. The use of the present participle may carry the idea that it is God's characteristic to give victory. This is daily victory. *Victory* is just one word, but it sums up all Paul has written in this chapter. It denotes enemies and a battle, but not ours. This great victory is being given to us by

God because of the Victor, "our Lord Jesus Christ," who is the medium through whom the victory becomes ours.

Paul closes this tremendous chapter with a practical exhortation to daily living in view of this great doctrine (v. 58). He applies the teaching to the unsettlement and unrest caused by the Corinthians' doubt. The effect of unbelief is now seen on Christian work. "Wherefore" *(ASV)* brings the matter to the point of conclusion and application. "My beloved brethren" not only shows Paul's concern for them; it also calls on them to prove themselves brothers. They are urged negatively not to be flighty, movable, or unstable in their Christian beliefs and actions, but steadfast and unmovable. There is the idea of a rocklike purpose. Positively, they are urged to be "abounding" or overflowing in the work of the Lord.

Paul states what he has been so strongly implying: We should work abundantly in the Lord's work because our labor is not in vain. What a fitting conclusion to this section! What assurance and incentive! Our labor "in the Lord" is not illusion, not profitless but profitable, rewarding, promised success, which should spur us to greater work. What an inspiration to weariness and discouragement. We shall not stand with empty hands when the labor is ended. We have "victory in Jesus!"

VIII

General Instructions
and Greetings
(16:1-24)

A. The Collection (Offering) for Jerusalem (16:1-9)

With the opening of this chapter Paul has almost completed his letter. Items of large importance have been discussed, the last major item being the doctrine of the resurrection. Now Paul has a few general items he wishes to quickly mention before closing. They are not lengthy but they are needful reminders. So, very quickly, he passes over several items.

He first touches on the offering to be taken for Jerusalem (v. 1). Paul was very sympathetic to the plight of his own countrymen in Jerusalem who had been in such a severe economic shortage. He had also made a promise concerning them (Galatians 2:10). But further, Paul saw in this time of need a chance to unite the Jewish and Gentile elements of the Church. By this Gentile expression, the Jews would realize their genuine love and faith in Christ. For these reasons Paul urges this collection for Jerusalem.

The large number of poor Christians in Jerusalem was not due only to the practice of the community of goods, as recorded in Acts 4:32-37. There was also a great deal of persecution and ostracism of Christians. This is, in passing, an Early Church example of world missions and how to fulfill that responsibility. With this in mind, we turn to the text.

"Now concerning" (v. 1) introduces a new topic. It is also the phrase used, as we have noted, to mark topics mentioned by the Corinthians in their letter to Paul. There is an implied principle of giving here. Paul has just closed his tremendous chapter on the resurrection. He immediately goes to this collection for the saints. It must come from the highest motives. It was a part "of the work

161

of the Lord" in which Christians are to abound because of their victory through the Lord Jesus Christ.

This collection was most important to Paul, as we have already seen, and was being made throughout the Gentile churches (at least those Paul had founded), as can be seen by the reference "to the churches of Galatia."[231] The fact that this collection was being made for the saints should recommend it to saints wherever they are.

Paul gives principles by which this collection was to be made (v. 2). He desired that it be generous and systematic. This is why he took a little more time in gathering it. The giving was to be systematically arranged, on the "first day of the week"; not on a hit-and-miss system, but regularly. This is a clear support for the habitual observance of that day (Sunday) from the time of the apostles. It was a weekly commemoration of the resurrection of the Lord Jesus Christ and shows the tremendous importance attached to that event. It is also an indication of the importance of the habitual fellowship of the saints in worship.

Paul adds another principle. Everyone should make a contribution. This is not to be based on age, prosperity, or status. Each should give something, however small or large. Many have suggested that "lay by him in store" means each was to keep his money at home in savings. This has some strong support; yet Paul wanted no offerings when he came, which would seem to be necessary if each one had stored his money at home. The church treasury would serve this purpose well.

Each one is to give proportionately. No definite percentage or amount is mentioned. Some could give more and some less. At this point it is left to the individual. The only qualification Paul makes is that each give as "God hath prospered him."[232] A man's giving should be in direct proportion to the way he is prospering.

Yet another principle surfaces in this verse. The emphasis is on regular giving rather than occasional emotional appeals. Paul wants no "gatherings" (of money) when he comes. *Gatherings* is the same Greek word as is translated "collection" in verse 1. Paul uses the indefinite *when,* for the particulars of his coming are uncertain. Paul desires to be able to devote himself to higher matters of teaching, etc., and not to spend his time gathering this collection.

Another New Testament principle of giving appears in verse 3. These financial gifts must be carefully administered. Reputable, honest, trusted individuals were to be picked by the Corinthians to carry these funds to the Jerusalem church. This is an area of the church that needs great care and any hint of suspicion or mismanagement must be guarded against. This arrangement would also protect Paul from the accusation of an unhealthy interest in the offering. Moreover, those who did the giving should be able to send their gift. And this trip would bring the Corinthians into personal contact with the Jerusalem believers and strengthen the unity of the Church. There is nothing corresponding to "your" in the Greek and the comma may come after "approve"; the idea being that after the Corinthians had picked men for this responsibility, Paul would write letters of commendation to be sent with them. This was to be a loving and gracious gift in a loving and gracious spirit to the needy at Jerusalem.

A thought is added on the possibility of Paul going to Jerusalem with those who will carry this gift (v. 4). Paul inserts "if" because he is uncertain as to whether or not he will go. The idea is that if the amount given is worthy, then Paul would supervise its delivery to these in need. The giving of Christians should be such as to note the blessings of Christ and their own proper stewardship of the things of this earth. They are to be generously given and shared, not hoarded; because earthly possessions are but temporal. Paul is not certain of the liberality of the Corinthians, thus he is guarding his position as an apostle, and his self-respect.

Verses 5-9 attach so naturally with verse 4 that it does not seem necessary to divide the thought. Paul declares that he will come to visit them, although at the time of this writing the date is uncertain. In 4:18, 19, Paul had remarked on those who did not think he would actually come to them. Now he states the fact with certainty. The time is set as "when I shall pass through Macedonia." "When" is indefinite again. "Pass through" regularly denotes in Acts an evangelistic tour. The last part of this verse appears to give new information to the readers, as though they had not known before of Paul's trip.

But Paul does not wish to just visit Corinth in passing. Rather, he desires to abide with them awhile (v. 6). Both "it may be" and "whithersoever I go" indicate clear uncertainty as to the apostle's future plans. Winter was the time when travel was normally suspended. This extended visit during the winter would allow the Corinthians opportunity to "bring [Paul] on [his] journey." In other words, it would give them a chance to provide what he had need of for the journey. "You" is emphatic. It is interesting that this is what Paul finally did. Acts 20:1-3 records that he traveled from Ephesus to Macedonia, and after "much exhortation" he went to Greece where he stayed for 3 months.

But Paul will not do this immediately. He does not wish to make a quick visit (v. 7). The "now" does not support a prior brief visit by Paul. The Corinthians had requested his speedy arrival and this could have been arranged. He could have visited Corinth on his way to Macedonia. But such a visit could only have been "by the way," in passing. There was much to be done at Corinth, and such a quick visit would have been of little help. But always there remained a greater leading than the apostle's own wish and will. That was the Lord's will; "if the Lord permit." Paul was above all a servant and he went where his Master, the Lord, directed. There was always the possibility the Lord would lead him elsewhere. This had happened to Paul on other occasions.

Paul, in connection with this, explains when he will leave Ephesus and gives a brief testimony concerning his work there. His present, continuing work was at Ephesus and he must stay there until it was completed. He would remain until Pentecost, the "fiftieth day" from the 16th Nisan in the Passover Feast. "Door" is a figurative expression. "Effectual" is unusual here, especially in regard to its modification of door. It means "active" or "effective," and speaks of the influence gained by entering. "Great" speaks of the door's width and the region into which it opens. "Is opened" indicates present and continuous opportunity. But Paul also calls his readers' attention to the fact of great opposition. Acts 19 expresses the extent of the adversity. Wherever the work of the Lord goes forth, it increases and flourishes in the midst of opposition and adversity. That is part of its character; it is also part of its marvel. For Paul is persuaded of (and history records) his victory (in Christ).

B. The Visits of Timothy and Apollos (16:10-12)

Paul has just stated that it would not be wise or helpful for him to visit Corinth at this time. It could be only a quick visit and that was not the type of trip desired. So he would come later. But others would visit Corinth now. Paul had urged Apollos to visit Corinth, but for reasons not clearly elucidated here, he had declined (v. 12). But even with "if," it appears Timothy would come, and on that premise Paul gives direction on Timothy's visit and Apollos' intentions.

Paul puts in a word for his young assistant Timothy (v. 10). It would appear from Acts 19:22, that Timothy traveled with Erastus and they journeyed to Macedonia first. It is a possibility that Paul was unsure that Timothy would reach Corinth, but his "if" need not imply uncertainty. Some others translate this "when." The first view is strongly argued. Local circumstances in Macedonia or even the reported unfriendliness of the Corinthians could have kept Timothy from Corinth. He is noted with Paul in Macedonia some time later when 2 Corinthians is written. There is no specific reference there to Timothy's visit to Corinth in the interval before, but it appears Titus had visited there. The second interpretation has had some grounds of support also, for Timothy is closely associated with Paul in regard to the problems at Corinth in the second Epistle. Perhaps it was through Timothy that Paul was grieved and insulted by a certain Corinthian Christian.[233]

Paul's direction to make Timothy at ease points to the disposition both of Timothy and the Corinthian church (vv. 10, 11). It points to Timothy's youth, sensitivity, and possibly his timidity. On the other hand, it also reveals the confidence, self-willedness, and unloving, inhospitable nature of the church at Corinth. Paul was concerned that Timothy might not be able to deal adequately with such difficulties. Therefore, Paul reminds his readers that he and Timothy are engaged in the same work: "the work of the Lord." They have the same purpose, the same calling, and the same Lord and Master. If Timothy attempted the task of 1 Corinthians 4:17, there was the possibility of trouble. In that situation some might attack Timothy's youth and calling. Paul urges them not to do so.

Rather, Timothy is to be sent forward on his journey in peace. "Conduct him forth" uses the same verb as that in verse 6, of Paul being sent on his journey. The Corinthians were to arrange and

165

obtain that which was necessary for Timothy's journey. It appears Paul expected Timothy's return before he departed from Ephesus.

It is difficult to tell whether "with the brethren" should join with the subject, "I with the brethren," or the object, "I await him with [and] the brethren." If it is the former, "the brethren" would probably refer to those of verses 12-18, the Corinthian brethren now visiting Ephesus and interested in Timothy's report. They would be delaying their return until they had heard his report. This would suggest a further reason why the Corinthian church should send Timothy back "in peace." If the latter view is accepted, "the brethren" would refer to those, possibly such as Erastus, who were expected to arrive from Corinth with Timothy. Most interpreters accept this. However, the implication of the scriptural context would seem to support the first view; but this is impossible to assert with absolute certainty.

Paul also adds a word concerning Apollos (v. 12). Paul's use of the phrase "as touching . . . Apollos" suggests that his coming had been mentioned in the Corinthian letter to Paul. Considering the factions in Corinth and the fact that Apollos was viewed as a rival of Paul's there, it was gracious of Paul to urge him to go to Corinth. This speaks of Paul's loving and forgiving nature and also indicates his opinion of the church's foolish and damaging disunity. (For "with the brethren" see verse 11.)

Apollos did not choose to come at that time. This points to his intention to be completely clear in the matter and to do nothing to increase the factional spirit at Corinth. It also shows a consideration for his fellow servants; in this case, particularly Paul. It should be mentioned that there are those who conclude that Apollos was simply too busy to come at the time Paul approached him. It does seem Apollos was not in Ephesus at the time of Paul's writing. Perhaps he had already left to do the business that occupied him. But Apollos would come when he had the opportunity and convenient time.

C. The Charge to Steadfastness (16:13, 14)

At this point Paul gives some positive charges for the Corinthians to live and act by. These short, decisive, powerful phrases

166

ring like military charges from a commander to his troops. They are clear, commanding, and charged with direction.

Paul places the responsibility squarely on the shoulders of the Corinthians themselves (v. 13). It is not only for Paul or the other apostles and leaders to be thus; it is also needful for every man to be so minded. "Watch ye!" *Watch* is a present imperative. He is speaking of a continuing state. All the imperatives, in fact, in these two verses are present imperatives. More is meant here than the mere absence of sleep. There is the idea of determined wakefulness and alertness. This is an appeal against the heedlessness of the Corinthians. In Scripture there is both the warning to watchfulness against temptation and sin, and for the second coming of the Lord. The tone and instruction of this admonitory section is found earlier in 1 Corinthians 15:58. Paul desires that the Christian man be spiritually watchful and alert.

Such stability and steadfastness as Paul urges was often lacking among the Corinthians; so this appeal comes against their fickleness. They should not be blown about as straw in the wind with the appeals and challenges of the pagans around them. They should be as trees with deep and ever-deepening roots. (Similar admonitions are found in Joshua 23:7, 8; Philippians 1:27; 1 Peter 5:9; 2 Peter 3:17.) Numerous examples of steadfastness are also found. But Paul directs them to a particular steadfastness: "Stand fast *in the faith*"; in the person and power of Jesus Christ and His love. (In conjunction with this thought, note 13:2, 13 and 15:14-17, which mention "faith.")

Further, they are to be mature and courageous. There is a challenge to "play the man" *(Moffatt)* and actively accomplish the Christian life. It is a charge against the childishness of the Corinthians. They have not been able to succeed because of their entanglement with heathen society and influence. But this fight over sin and opposition of every sort is not one for children; it is for men. This is a charge for every Christian.

Paul instructs his readers to be strong. It is often during such charges to strength that we feel weakest. But this is the time to go to the Strong One for strength. The Lion of Judah can give lionlike strength. We must "be mighty" in Christian activity, by the power of the Lord. This opposes the Corinthians' tendency to moral weakness and unsteadiness.

167

With the charge to love we are returned to 1 Corinthians 8 and 13, for their great descriptions of love (16:14). The Greek better states "in love." This refers to *agape* love, the highest, complete love. It stands here as more than an equal or companion to Christian action; it is the realm and atmosphere within which the Christian thinks, moves, and lives. It is the fountain out of which flow all proper actions. This admonition touches on the great underlying problem at Corinth—their lack of love—and is in the vein of 1 Peter 4:8. Such love must, can, and will flow to and out of the Christian from the Lord, for "God is love."

D. Respect for the "Local" Ministry (16:15-18)

Paul had received a group of visitors from Corinth. Most likely they had brought the Corinthian letter to him. Three of this party were Stephanas, Fortunatus, and Achaicus, all probably leaders in the Corinthian church (note 1:16). They had tarried in Ephesus to visit at length with Paul, who had been singularly impressed, inspired, refreshed by them. In commenting on these enjoyable men in closing his letter, Paul takes the opportunity to remind the Corinthians that such men should be honored, respected, and acknowledged for their stand and work.

Paul sets before the Corinthians men to pattern themselves after (v. 15). In the midst of an Epistle that has of necessity dealt with numerous negative issues, Paul positively notes the excellent example of the household of Stephanas. They already held a special joy for Paul; he had baptized them. Now we are told they are the firstfruits of the province. This province included Athens, and Paul had made some converts there before he preached at Corinth. So what does he mean here? It may be the household of Stephanas had been somehow converted before Paul ministered in Athens, or when he did so. Or, it may be this was the first household converted, in contrast with individuals. Or, maybe Paul means by "firstfruits" those fruits that give promise of a future harvest. This household had "addicted themselves to the ministry of the saints." *Addicted* was used, for example, by Plato of certain individuals who worked at the business of serving the public by retailing farm produce. This household of Stephanas had set themselves the responsibility of Christian service, of "ministry." *Ministry* is a general word, not indicating clergy, but representing service. "Saints" cannot refer to the Jerusalem saints of verse 1. The word *ministry* is too general and the surrounding idea is of much service. Stephanas' trip to Ephesus with the church letter may be an example of such service.

Paul notes the manner in which the Corinthians are to treat such as the house of Stephanas (v. 16). Again the indication does not seem to be a specific order of church officials. Paul is asking them for willing submission to the direction of those willing and able to lead in profitable and excellent work. Paul speaks much about Christians being submissive to one another, in opposition to our natural tendencies. Such extensive work and sacrifice deserves and earns respect and leadership in the Christian church. *Us* is absent in the Greek. Paul includes in this sweeping statement not only the house of Stephanas, but also all who do such help and labor in the church. All these deserve to be heeded in their counsel, respected, and looked up to.

Paul admonishes the Corinthians about their manner toward such as Stephanas when they arrive home. But at present, he expresses his joy over their being with him (vv. 17, 18). He adds the names of Fortunatus and Achaicus to that of Stephanas. Fortunatus was a common Latin name. Achaicus was a rare Greek name. Due to their names, some have supposed one or both were slaves, although there is little to support this. These three probably carried the church letter. And since Paul commends them at the close of this letter, it is possible they will carry his letter back to Corinth.

It may be Paul is saying that these three had made up to him for the absence of the Corinthians (v. 17). In other words, they had representatively supplied him with the desired fellowship of the Corinthians. Or, it may mean the supposed desire for access to Paul had been representatively supplied by these from Corinth. The former seems more reasonable since they could more easily supply Paul's need here than Corinth's. It also fits Paul's nature and satisfies "coming." It notes the tenderness and depth of his feeling for the Corinthians even though they had not always treated him in a fitting or proper manner.

The coming of these emissaries had been enjoyable not only because they had supplied a need, but also because they had

169

refreshed Paul's spirit and, therefore, also that of the Corinthians. Paul realizes that his own comfort and refreshment will affect his friends in Corinth. It will please and cheer them to know this visit had such desirable effects. Men such as these are to be acknowledged and respected. Again the outlook includes not just Stephanas and his group but all such men in the Church.

E. The Salute of the Churches (and Brethren) (16:19, 20)

Paul delighted in binding all the various churches together with expressions of love. That is what he does here with these greetings to the Corinthians. There are greetings from the churches of Asia, not just of Ephesus. There are greetings from Aquila and Priscilla, and those who met in their home for worship. The third greeting is from "all the brethren." In response to this Christian brotherhood and affection, the readers were to express their fellowship by a "holy kiss." The Church is a unit and is to acknowledge and love the brethren everywhere.

Paul generally mentions the churches of Asia and specifically notes Aquila and Priscilla and those with them (v. 19). "Asia" refers to what was then the Roman province of Asia, and what is now western Asia Minor. Paul had not visited all these communities, but he was in contact with them and knew their desires toward the Corinthians. Aquila and Priscilla are mentioned in Acts 18:1-3. The Corinthians knew them well.

Aquila, a Jew, was originally from Pontus on the southern shore of the Black Sea. He had lived in Rome, but when the Emperor Claudius expelled all the Jews from Rome in about A.D. 49, he moved to Corinth. When Paul first came to Corinth he worked and lodged with them. Their generosity is again shown here. Their home had been placed at Paul's disposal and now we read of a church meeting there. (Note also Romans 16:3-5.) Furthermore, at some time they had risked their lives for him. They had also instructed and encouraged Apollos in the faith. The couple is mentioned six times in the New Testament and four times Priscilla's name is first, which indicates that she was exceptional in her own right.

"Salute you much" is a very deep, warm, affectionate Christian greeting. "With the church . . . in their house" can hardly mean the whole Ephesian church. Perhaps it means a neighboring section of it.

Paul adds a comprehensive salute and then indicates the proper response. "All the brethren" (v. 20) is not specific and therefore not clear, but it appears all-inclusive. The admonition from Paul on a "holy kiss" has caused much discussion. The custom was much more common then than now. Such a greeting would be a rebuke to any division or haughtiness; it would note that they were in accord. (There are other scriptural references to this: Romans 16:16; 2 Corinthians 13:12; 1 Thessalonians 5:26; 1 Peter 5:14.)

F. The Salutation and Benediction (16:21-24)

Paul closes with his personal signature and a very warm benediction. He has had much to say to these Corinthian readers. Some of the toughest church difficulties in the New Testament have been considered here. Yet Paul dearly loves these people and he wants to close in love. Therefore, very solemnly he announces the great curse or the great blessing open to them all and bows out with the greatest of all themes, the grace of Jesus Christ, and a gentle reminder of his love for them in Christ Jesus.

It was Paul's custom, for whatever reason, to dictate his letters to an amanuensis. But to mark the letter's genuineness he would, at the end, sign and close it himself (v. 21). This is what he does here. He makes it clear that this is his letter and his personal greeting.

With great feeling, Paul imparts a motto of judgment or blessing (v. 22). A comparison passage is found in Galatians 6:12-17. The first clause is: "If any man love not the Lord Jesus Christ, let him be Anathema. . . ." Paul displays a contradiction to some silent assertion. If a man pretends to love the Lord, but falsely or spuriously does so, let him be "Anathema." Such a one is accursed. "Love not" is a strong, deep note of accusation. It declares the individual to be heartless, lacking even human affection for Jesus. A notable example was Judas Iscariot and his traitorous kiss. Such men, as John points out, neither love nor know God.

The second clause is: "Maranatha." This is an Aramaic word translated into Greek. Dividing the word, it breaks down roughly

171

like this: *Mar* means "Lord"; *an* or *ana* denotes "our"; and the latter part is from the verb *atha,* which means "to come."[234] Some have translated this as strictly past: "Our Lord hath come." However, it seems better to translate it: "Our Lord cometh (will come, is at hand)." There are several reasons for supporting this latter interpretation. It is in accord with other Scripture passages (such as Philippians 4:5; 1 Thessalonians 4:14; James 5:7; Revelation 1:7; 3:11; 22:20). It fits the immediate context; it is in harmony with 1 Corinthians 15; and it agrees with the New Testament attitude toward Christ's return. Such phrases as this might have served as watchwords or even, under certain circumstances, as passwords among the early Christians.[235]

Paul desires that they be constantly attended by the marvelous grace of "our Lord Jesus Christ," and that it be the constant source of ministry and blessing to them. This was a common farewell from Paul and is expanded in 2 Corinthians 13:14. But Paul also adds a note of affection peculiar to this letter (v. 24) and yet fitting in light of some of the harsh directives he has had to give in this Epistle. He notes his love for them all; and he desires it in an abiding sense, "with you." He further notes the foundation and bond for love among them all—the bond of Jesus Christ. Division, bigotry, and non-Christian behavior were all products of the Corinthians' living. Much of it had been directed toward the apostle himself. Yet he still desires that his love be with them.

With these words the Epistle closes. It is only fitting that the last words should show the great heart of the apostle and, even more important, the bond of all things—the person of Jesus Christ. *Amen* is not in the best manuscripts. It is the kind of addition that naturally tends to be added. Paul's last word is *Jesus*. To which we add, "Amen."

Notes

Chapter I

[1]Romans 1:7; 2 Corinthians 1:2; Galatians 1:3; Ephesians 1:2; Philippians 1:2; Colossians 1:2; 1 Thessalonians 1:1; 2 Thessalonians 1:2; 1 Timothy 1:2; 2 Timothy 1:2; Titus 1:4; Philemon 3.

[2]W. Robertson Nicoll, ed., *The Expositor's Greek New Testament,* Vol. 2 (Grand Rapids: Wm. B. Eerdmans Pub. Co., 1952), p. 761.

[3]This fellowship κοινωνίαν may refer to subjective ("with," Philippians 1:5—alternate inferred reading from the Greek) or objective ("in" or "into," Philippians 3:10—alternate inferred reading from the Greek) fellowship. The subjective would seem to be best because nowhere else is this noun used as the objective genitive of person, and the reference in context seems to be to communion of which Christ is the sum.

Chapter II

[4]"Name" implied ownership, fellowship, allegiance. Paul did nothing to develop such a relationship with those he led to Christ.

[5] ἀπολλυμένοις —Dat. pl., masc., part., pres., pass.—are being brought to nothing, are being destroyed.

[6] σωζομένοις—Dat., pl., masc., part., pres., pass.—are being saved, rescued, preserved from harm.

[7]John 1:46; 7:47ff.; Acts 4:25-27; 1 Corinthians 2:8.

[8]Nicoll, *The Expositor's Greek New Testament,* p. 771.

[9]In "things" the neuter concentrates on the quality of foolishness possessed rather than on the individuals themselves (Morris, *Tyndale New Testament Commentaries,* Vol. 7 (Grand Rapids: Wm. B. Eerdmans Pub. Co., 1958), p. 48.

[10] δικαιοσύνη refers specifically to Paul's doctrine of justification by faith and speaks of a law court where the verdict is "not guilty" or "righteous." See Romans 3:24-26.

[11] ἁγιασμὸς refers to the continuous process of holiness and perfection as we remain in Christ. See John 17:19; Hebrews 10:10.

[12] ἀπολύτρωσις refers to deliverance by ransom, as when slaves are liberated with a purchase price. It may refer to the whole work of salvation, but it has special emphasis on the consummation of redemption. (Nicoll, *The Expositor's Greek New Testament,* p. 774.)

[13]"Lord" refers to Christ, as noted by context.

[14]It is not necessary to distinguish between "speech" (v. 4) and "preaching" as having the former refer to personal witness and the latter to group speaking. Paul is making a simple remark concerning his total presentation.

173

¹⁵This may refer to physical illness, but more probably is a description of Paul's feeling of inadequacy in himself.

¹⁶An inward emotion expressing "fear of failure."

¹⁷ τρόμῳ —used to describe the anxiety of one who distrusts his ability completely to meet all requirements, but does his utmost to fulfill his duty. (Joseph H. Thayer, *Greek-English Lexicon of the New Testament* [Grand Rapids: Zondervan Publishing House], 1962.)

¹⁸"Princes" (v. 8) would have to include the Jews, for as those who crucified Christ, they are representative of the world's rulers in general.

¹⁹"Heart" (v. 9) does not stand for the emotions. Among the Greeks the seat of the emotions was the intestines. Heart καρδίαν stood for the whole of a man's inner life, although at times one part was inclined toward. Perhaps the best word here would be *mind*. (Morris, *Tyndale New Testament Commentaries*, Vol. 7, pp. 56, 57.)

²⁰This may also be the work of the Spirit at salvation. It is impossible to say dogmatically.

²¹ πνευματικοῖς —"Thoughts, opinions, precepts, maxims, ascribable to the Holy Spirit working in the soul." This word is thus neuter "for Paul in delivering the things disclosed to him by the Holy Spirit in speech derived not from rhetorical instruction but received from the same divine Spirit, 'combines spiritual things with spiritual,' adapts the discourse to the subject" (Thayer, *Greek-English Lexicon of the New Testament*, pp. 523, 593).

²²This phrase has been interpreted as: (a) with the KJV, forming them into a correlated system; (b) proving spiritual things by spiritual, or the Old Testament proved by the New Testament; (c) adapting spiritual things to spiritual men, a strain on the verb; (d) interpreting spiritual things to spiritual men, misses emphasis of v. 13; (e) combining spiritual things with spiritual words *(ASV)*. The first (a) seems the strongest because: (1) According to Moulton and Milligan the first meaning of συγκρίνω is "to compare"; (2) πνευματικοῖς lacks the article; (3) Paul speaks here of contents of the words and of the way in which they are spoken, not of the people to whom they are spoken (Nicoll, *The Expositor's Greek New Testament*, p. 783; Frederick W. Grosheide, *Commentary on First Corinthians* (NIC) [Grand Rapids: Wm. B. Eerdmans Publishing Co., 1953], p. 72, footnote 24). This is Paul's rejoinder to those who thought his ideas and speech weak. Argument (e) might also be strongly argued for, although not as successfully as (a).

²³The first word is σαρκίνοις the second σαρκικοί .

²⁴"Divisions" is not in the more reliable manuscripts.

²⁵The two major views on "through whom you believed" (v. 5) are (a) ingressive aorist, "came to believe," and (b) constative—summing up the entire activity of believing (Richard C. Lenski, *The Interpretation of First & Second Corinthians* [Minneapolis: Augsburg Publishing House, 1935], p. 126).

²⁶This may mean either "with God" or fellow workers who belong to God and are working with one another. The first lends dignity to Christian service, but the second is to be preferred because it seems to fit best with the context and Paul's words on ministry (Leon Morris, *Tyndale New Testament Commentaries*, Vol. 7 [Grand Rapids: Wm. B. Eerdmans Publishing Co.], p. 66; Erdman, *The First Epistle of Paul to the Corinthians* [Philadelphia: Westminster Press, 1966], p. 47).

²⁷"Husbandry" may signify the field, process of cultivation, or imply the organic growth of the Church. See next footnote.

²⁸"Building" may suggest the edifice, the process of erection, or "the mutual adaptation of its parts." In the cases of both "husbandry" and "building," the

second meaning seems preferable because building in this light seems to fit better with the following five verses, and husbandry seems to fit at least partially with building. We would then conclude it is God's work in cultivation and building (Nicoll, *The Expositor's Greek New Testament,* p. 789).

[29]Matthew Henry, *Commentary on the Whole Bible,* Vol. 6 (Old Tappan, NJ: Fleming H. Revell), p. 518.

[30]"By fire" διὰ πυρός is proverbial for a hairbreadth escape, a very close, perilous, narrow escape, not necessarily without injury. The figure then is different somewhat from the figure in verse 13.

[31]The word ἱερόν included all the courts and structures on Temple Hill. But ναός, the word used in v. 16, referred to the structure containing the Holy Place and the Holy of Holies (Lenski, *The Interpretation of First & Second Corinthians,* p. 146).

[32]John 14:28; 20:17; 1 Corinthians 11:3; 15:23-28.

[33]This term ὑπηρέτας *ministers* applied generally to an "under-rower or one who rowed in the lower bank of oars on a large ship. It came to signify service, though generally of a lower kind and often with the hands" (Morris, *Tyndale New Testament Commentaries,* Vol. 7, p. 74).

[34]This term οἰκονόμους refers to the overseer of an estate.

[35]Grosheide, *Commentary on First Corinthians,* p. 102.

[36]Lenski, *The Interpretation of First & Second Corinthians,* p. 179.

[37]This refers to the rubbish heap or the mass of sweepings and litter gathered together when one cleans up (*Ibid.,* p. 190).

[38]This is that which is removed by scouring a filthy object.

[39]This does not refer to a schoolmaster, but to a nursery governor who had charge of a child from his tender years, looking after his food, dress, speech, and manners, and when old enough taking the child to and from school (Nicoll, *The Expositor's Greek New Testament,* pp. 799-806).

[40]Grosheide says "power" (v. 19) is not the power to perform miracles but the power of a genuine Christian life. Calvin adds that it would include "that spiritual efficacy, with which those are endowed who dispense the word of the Lord with earnestness" (Grosheide, *Commentary on First Corinthians,* p. 115; and Morris, *Tyndale New Testament Commentaries,* Vol. 7, p. 85).

Chapter III

[41]Leviticus 18:7ff; Deuteronomy 22:30.

[42]Morris, *Tyndale New Testament Commentaries,* Vol. 7, p. 86.

[43]*Ibid.,* p. 87.

[44]Verses 3-5 are actually one long, difficult sentence in the Greek, with it being necessary to sort out dependence and association of the different phrases.

[45]2 Corinthians 4:4; Ephesians 2:2; 6:12; Colossians 1:13; 1 Timothy 1:20.

[46]Nicoll, *The Expositor's Greek New Testament,* p. 809.

[47]"Within" and "without" denoted in synagogue usage members and nonmembers of the sacred community (*Ibid.,* p. 813).

[48]This follows a similar Rabbinical inhibition: "It is forbidden to bring a matter

of right before idolatrous judges. . . . Whosoever goeth before them with a lawsuit is impious, and does the same as though he blasphemed and cursed; and hath lifted his hand against the law of Moses our Teacher, blessed be he!" (*Ibid.*, p. 814).

[49]Grosheide, *Commentary on First Corinthians,* p. 138.

[50]Matthew 20:25-28; John 13:13-20, 34, 35.

[51]Grosheide, *Commentary on First Corinthians,* p. 140.

[52]John 8:34; Romans 6:16, 20.

[53]Nicoll, *The Expositor's Greek New Testament,* p. 818.

[54]Morris, *Tyndale New Testament Commentaries,* Vol. 7, p. 100.

[55]This is the only such expression in this Epistle.

[56] κολλώμενος ("joined") in v. 17 is used of close bonds of various kinds. Literally, it refers to the process of glueing. It points to a very close tie (Morris, *Tyndale New Testament Commentaries,* Vol. 7, p. 102). It should also be noted that "joined" in v. 16 and v. 17 is the same Greek word in each case.

[57]Mark 7:18-23.

[58]Morris, *Tyndale New Testament Commentaries,* Vol. 7, p. 104.

[59]The words after "body" in v. 20 are absent from the better manuscripts. They express truth, but are not part of the text. The context concerns the body, not the spirit.

Chapter IV

[60]"Fasting" (v. 5) is absent from the better manuscripts.

[61]1 Corinthians 7:33-40; 1 Peter 3:7.

[62]"This" in v. 6 cannot refer to either v. 4 or 5 because they do not fit "concession." But vv. 2, 3 do, and they express the main thought. Verses 4, 5 only add explanation. Most commentators agree on this.

[63]This theme will be enlarged in 1 Corinthians 12.

[64] τοὶς is masculine.

[65]Acts 20:35; 1 Corinthians 7:10; 9:14; 1 Thessalonians 4:15.

[66]On "not the wife depart" ("not to be separated"), Moulton and Milligan say in the papyri this became almost a technical term in connection with divorce (*Vocabulary of the Greek New Testament* [Grand Rapids: Wm. B. Eerdmans Publishing Co., 1949]).

[67]Observe 2 Corinthians 6:14, 15.

[68]Morris, *Tyndale New Testament Commentaries,* Vol. 7, p. 109.

[69]See 1 Corinthians 6:16, 17.

[70]Genesis 15:18; 17:7; 18:26; 1 Kings 15:4; Isaiah 37:4.

[71]"Depart" is in the middle voice—"take himself off."

[72]Romans 12:18; Galatians 5:22.

[73]Grosheide, *Commentary on First Corinthians,* p. 167.

[74]Nicoll, *The Expositor's Greek New Testament,* pp. 827, 828.

[75]1 Thessalonians 4:11, 12; 2 Thessalonians 3:6-15.

[76]Margaret E. Thrall, *First & Second Letters of Paul to the Corinthians* (New English Bible Commentaries) (New Rochelle, NY: Cambridge University Press, 1965), p. 55.

[77]Morris, *Tyndale New Testament Commentaries,* Vol. 7, p. 114.

[78]*Ibid.,* p. 115.

[79]"Good for a man so to be" ὅτι καλὸν ἀνθρώπῳ τὸ οὕτως ἐιναι (v. 26) is open to one of three constructions; as ὅτι is rendered that, because, or which ὅ,τι : (1) Make the clause an expanded restatement of τουτο καλὸν ὑπάρχειν , "I think then this to be good . . . that it is good (I say) for a man to remain as he is;" (2) make it the ground, based on v. 1—"I think this to be good (in their case) . . . because it is good for one . . . to remain as one is," . . . single; (3) attach ὅ,τι to the antecedent τοῦτο and defining it by the subsequent τ. οὕτως ἐιναι —"I think this to be good (in the case of maidens) because of the present straits, which is good (as I have said, I) for one generally, viz., to remain unmarried." The first seems best because of the ground and view of verse 1 and because Paul appears to open his advice to both sexes. Grammatically then he speaks conversationally, placing ὅτι καλού κ.τ.λ. in apposition: "I think this to be good because of the present straits . . . yes that it is good . . . (for anyone . . .) not to change one's state" (Nicoll, *The Expositor's Greek New Testament,* pp. 831, 832).

[80]Revelation 22:20.

[81]Nicoll, *The Expositor's Greek New Testament,* pp. 831, 832.

[82]Paul may add "and is divided" (vv. 33, 34). There are arguments both ways and a complicated issue results. The reference of phrases here however does not affect the context or meaning and thus I have chosen not to discuss it here.

[83]"Snare" (v. 35) βρόχος is the noose or lasso by which a wild creature is snared. Paul does not wish to deprive the Corinthians of their liberty nor force them to celibacy (Nicoll, *The Expositor's Greek New Testament,* p. 836).

[84]Morris, *Tyndale New Testament Commentaries,* Vol. 7, pp. 120-122.

[85]It could also point to some outward situation such as a marriage agreement. The father is under no compulsion to change the plan for any reason, perhaps even financial.

[86]"Shall do" is future, indicating that what Paul was writing about had not yet taken place. This also suggests that the outcome prove the fact.

Chapter V

[87]Paul uses the perfect tense of the verb, implying full and complete knowledge. Even then he does not know as he "ought to" or "must."

[88]Morris, *Tyndale New Testament Commentaries,* Vol. 7, p. 125.

[89]See also 2 Timothy 2:19; Galatians 4:9.

[90]"Is known" refers to a knowledge that has reached its peak and is not capable of augmentation (Grosheide, *Commentary on First Corinthians,* p. 191).

[91]"No idol is anything" *(ASV).*

[92]See John 1:3; 2 Corinthians 5:18; Ephesians 1:5; Hebrews 1:2.

[93]In verse 1 Paul says knowledge is not confined to a certain group in Corinth. But that does not mean all Christians possessed it.

[94]Goodspeed translates, "through being long accustomed to idols."

[95]This idea is based on the fact that pride might result from such a view and verse 9 appears as a warning to verse 8 (Grosheide, *Commentary on First Corinthians,* p. 194).

[96] πρόσκομμα (stumblingblock), v. 9 is something that lies in the path, which an unwary foot might strike and cause the person to stumble or fall; metaphorically it is anything that may cause one to sin and injure his soul (Lenski, *The Interpretation of First & Second Corinthians,* p. 344.)

[97]"Emboldened" is translated "edifieth" in v. 1. Paul speaks ironically. Perhaps these thought of "building" up by their poor example. The result was destruction instead.

[98]"Make . . . to offend" σκανδαλίζει is difficult to translate. It really means something like "to set off a trap." It comes from the word which means the stick which triggers a trap, or sets it in motion for bird or animal, when touched (Morris, *Tyndale New Testament Commentaries*, Vol. 7, p. 130).

[99]These opening questions are reversed in the better manuscripts.

[100]Acts 1:21ff; 2:32; 3:15; 4:33; 22:14.

[101]Morris, *Tyndale New Testament Commentaries*, Vol. 7, p. 132.

[102]Both "answer" and "examine" (v. 3) are legal words, as though defending against a charge.

[103]By Christ: the camp (Luke 11:21, 22; 14:31); the vineyard (Matthew 20:1; 21:28); the flock (Luke 12:32; John 10:1-16; 21:15). By Paul: the camp (1 Corinthians 14:8; Ephesians 6:10; 1 Thessalonians 5:8); the vineyard (1 Corinthians 3:6); the flock (Acts 20:28; Ephesians 4:11).

[104]"Bear all things," i.e., to cover by keeping silence (Grosheide, *Commentary on First Corinthians*, p. 207).

[105]"Hinder" (v. 12) means literally "a cutting into"; used of breaking up a road to prevent an enemy's advance. Used only here in the New Testament (Morris, *Tyndale New Testament Commentaries*, Vol. 7, pp. 135, 136).

[106]2 Corinthians 11:12; 12:17-19; 1 Thessalonians 2:5.

[107]The American Standard Version translates verse 20: "And to the Jews I became as a Jew, that I might gain Jews; to them that are under the law, as under the law, not being myself under the law, that I might gain them that are under the law."

[108]Note Philippians 3:7-14 for the inner side of this "one thing."

[109]Erdman, *The First Epistle of Paul to the Corinthians*, p. 99.

[110]Exodus 13:20-22; 14:19.

[111]Exodus 14.

[112]For a comparison of Moses and Christ, see Hebrews 3.

[113]Exodus 16:11-15.

[114]Exodus 17:1-7; Numbers 20:1-11.

[115]Numbers 14:30.

[116]Lenski, *The Interpretation of First & Second Corinthians*, p. 399.

[117]2 Samuel 24:16; Isaiah 37:36; Exodus 12:23; Hebrews 11:28.

[118]Morris, *Tyndale New Testament Commentaries*, Vol. 7, p. 145.

[119]Nicoll, *The Expositor's Greek New Testament*, pp. 864, 865.

[120]Leviticus 7:15, 16.

[121]The better manuscripts reverse the order of the questions in v. 19.

[122]2 Corinthians 4:4; Ephesians 2:2; 6:12; Luke 4:6; 1 John 5:19.

[123]See Deuteronomy 32:17.

[124]Grosheide, *Commentary on First Corinthians*, p. 240.

[125]Verse 26 is a quotation from Psalm 24:1.

[126]Grosheide, *Commentary on First Corinthians*, p. 241.

[127]The words that immediately follow in verse 28 are not in the better manuscripts.

Chapter VI

[128]This has the definite article denoting *the* Christ.

[129]Nicoll, *The Expositor's Greek New Testament*, p. 872.

[130]"For that is even all one . . . shaven" (v. 5) is better translated, "She is one and the same as the shaven one."

[131]Genesis 1:26, 27.

[132]The American Standard Version translates this, "a sign of authority on her head."

[133]Nicoll, *The Expositor's Greek New Testament*, p. 874.

[134]*Ibid.*

[135]Luke 2:13; 12:8; 15:10; Acts 1:10.

[136]1 Timothy 5:21; Ephesians 3:10.

[137]Morris, *Tyndale New Testament Commentaries*, Vol. 7, p. 154, footnote 1.

[138]*Ibid.*

[139] δεῖ (there) affirms necessity abiding in the present moral conditions. αἵρεσις (sects) implies mental tendency and from that "a sect or party formed on a basis of opinion" (Nicoll, *The Expositor's Greek New Testament*, p. 877).

[140]Grosheide, *Commentary on First Corinthians*, p. 266.

[141]G. Coleman Luck, *First Corinthians* (Chicago: Moody Press, 1967), p. 91.

[142] κλώμενον (broken) is not in the Greek text. Paul leaves the word to be supplied. Nor is "take, eat" in the better manuscripts.

[143] διακρίνω (discerning) is, one "discerns (judges clearly and rightly of) the (Lord's) body" in the sacrament, and "discriminates" it from all other eating and drinking (Nicoll, *The Expositor's Greek New Testament*, pp. 882, 883).

[144] κρίμα (damnation) means a judicial sentence of any kind and should be distinguished from κατάκριμα, the final condemnation of the sinner (v. 32) (*Ibid.*, p. 883). "Unworthily" is not in the text.

[145]Matthew 13:54; Mark 6:2; Luke 21:15; Acts 6:3, 10; 15:19-22; Romans 11:33; 1 Corinthians 1:30; Colossians 1:28; 2:3; 4:5; James 1:5; 3:13, 17; Revelation 17:9.

[146]Myer Pearlman, *Knowing the Doctrines of the Bible* (Springfield, MO: Gospel Publishing House, 1937), p. 322.

[147]Colossians 2:3; Hebrews 4:13.

[148]Ephesians 1:17-19; 2 Peter 3:18.

[149]1 Samuel 9:15, 16; 10:2, 21, 22; Acts 10:19,20.

[150]Donald Gee, *Spiritual Gifts in the Work of the Ministry Today* (Springfield, MO: Gospel Publishing House, 1963), p. 65.

[151]Acts 8:6, 7.

[152]Mark 16:18; James 5:14, 15.

[153]Acts 1:8; 5:12-15; 19:11, 12.

[154]Exodus 4:2-7; Acts 8:39, 40.

[155]Pearlman, *Knowing the Doctrines of the Bible*, p. 324.

[156]1 Corinthians 14:3.

[157]Romans 12:6-8; 1 Corinthians 14:24, 25, 31; Ephesians 2:21, 22.

[158]John 16:13; Acts 11:27, 28; 20:23; 21:10, 11.

[159]1 Corinthians 14:29.

[160]Luke 1:67-79; 1 Corinthians 14:14, 15.

179

[161]1 Thessalonians 5:19-22.

[162]John 1:47-50; 2:24, 25; Acts 5:3; 8:23; 13:6-12; 16:16-18.

[163]Acts 2:4; 1 Corinthians 12:30; 14:2-4.

[164]1 Corinthians 14:21, 22.

[165]1 Corinthians 14:5.

[166]Grosheide says that the aorist ἐποτίσθημεν is not to be taken of baptism but of the receiving of the Spirit at baptism (Acts 10:44-48; 19:5, 6) and that Paul has this historical fact in mind (Grosheide, *Commentary on First Corinthians*, p. 293, footnote 14).

[167]Erdman, *The First Epistle of Paul to the Corinthians*, p. 128.

[168]Henry, *Commentary on the Whole Bible*, p. 571.

[169]Acts 13:1; Ephesians 4:11.

[170]Morris, *Tyndale New Testament Commentaries*, Vol. 7, p. 180.

[171]Ephesians 4:1-3; 2 Peter 3:9.

[172]Luke 6:27-35; James 3:17.

[173]James 3:14-16.

[174]Proverbs 15:33; 16:19; 22:4; Matthew 6:5.

[175]1 Peter 3:8-11.

[176]1 Corinthians 10:33; Philippians 2:4.

[177]James 1:3, 4; 5:7.

[178]Proverbs 10:12; 1 Peter 4:8.

[179]John 14:6; Romans 14:17; Ephesians 4:21.

[180]Ephesians 4:2; Colossians 3:13.

[181]2 Thessalonians 1:4; Hebrews 6:15; 1 Peter 2:19.

[182]Morris, *Tyndale New Testament Commentaries*, Vol. 7, p. 188, footnote.

[183]Romans 5:2-5; Galatians 5:5ff; Colossians 1:4ff; 1 Thessalonians 1:3; 5:8; Hebrews 6:10-12; 1 Peter 1:21, 22.

[184]Nicoll, *The Expositor's Greek New Testament*, p. 901.

[185]Grosheide, *Commentary on First Corinthians*, p. 316.

[186]"Unknown" is not in the better manuscripts.

[187]Morris, *Tyndale New Testament Commentaries*, Vol. 7, p. 192.

[188]*Ibid.*, p. 195, A.G.

[189]Grosheide, *Commentary on First Corinthians*, p. 330.

[190]Morris, *Tyndale New Testament Commentaries*, Vol. 7, p. 199.

[191]Nicoll, *The Expositor's Greek New Testament*, p. 914.

[192]Grosheide, *Commentary on First Corinthians*, pp. 341, 342.

[193]Luck, *First Corinthians*, p. 111.

[194]Morris, *Tyndale New Testament Commentaries*, Vol. 7, p. 201.

[195]1 Corinthians 11:3; Galatians 5:13; Ephesians 5:22-33.

[196] ἀγνοεῖται instead of ἀγνοείτω.

[197]Matthew 7:22-29; 10:14-42; John 5:37-47; 13:20; 2 Timothy 2:19; 3 John 9-12.

Chapter VII

[198]Verses 12, 13, 14, 16, 17, 20. Morris, *Tyndale New Testament Commentaries*, Vol. 7, p. 206.

[199]Romans 3:23-26; 5:6-11; 2 Corinthians 5:18-21; Galatians 3:10ff.

[200]Lenski, *The Interpretation of First & Second Corinthians,* p. 634.

[201]Nicoll, *The Expositor's Greek New Testament,* p. 920.

[202]Galatians 1:19; 2:9, 12.

[203]Nicoll, *The Expositor's Greek New Testament,* p. 921.

[204]Acts 26:9-11; Galatians 1:13; 1 Timothy 1:12-15.

[205]Acts 2:36; 13:30-39; 17:31; Romans 1:4; Galatians 1:1; Ephesians 1:20.

[206]Morris, *Tyndale New Testament Commentaries,* Vol. 7, p. 213.

[207]Leviticus 23:10; Matthew 13:39; John 5:28ff.; Revelation 14:14-20 (Nicoll, *The Expositor's Greek New Testament,* p. 925).

[208]*Ibid.,* p. 928.

[209]*New Catholic Encyclopedia,* Vol. 2, edited by Wm. J. McDonald, et al. (New York: McGraw-Hill Book Co., 1967), p. 68.

[210]J. R. Clark, *On the Way to Immortality and Eternal Life* (Salt Lake City, 1950), pp. 187, 188.

[211]Charles Ellicott, *A Bible Commentary for English Readers,* Vol. 7 (London: Cassell and Co.), p. 349.

[212]Nicoll, *The Expositor's Greek New Testament,* p. 930.

[213]Henry, *Commentary on the Whole Bible,* p. 591.

[214]Nicoll, *The Expositor's Greek New Testament,* p. 931.

[215]Alvah Hovey, ed., *An American Commentary on the New Testament,* Vol. 5 (Philadelphia, 1887), p. 134.

[216]Adam Clarke, *Clarke's Commentary,* Vol. 2 (New York: Abingdon Press).

[217]John 15:18 to 16:22; 1 Corinthians 4:9-13; 2 Corinthians 4:8-18; 11:23-33.

[218]Grosheide, *Commentary on First Corinthians,* p. 375.

[219]Nicoll, *The Expositor's Greek New Testament,* p. 933.

[220]Morris, *Tyndale New Testament Commentaries,* Vol. 7, p. 221.

[221]Nicoll, *The Expositor's Greek New Testament,* p. 943.

[222] σῶμα (body) is never used elsewhere in Biblical Greek and rarely in classical Greek of inorganic bodies.

[223]Morris, *Tyndale New Testament Commentaries,* Vol. 7, p. 225.

[224]Nicoll, *The Expositor's Greek New Testament,* p. 935.

[225]*Ibid.,* pp. 936, 937.

[226]John 6:33; 11:25; Romans 8:10ff.; 2 Corinthians 4:14; Colossians 1:18; Revelation 1:5.

[227]The better manuscripts omit "the Lord."

[228]Morris, *Tyndale New Testament Commentaries,* Vol. 7, p. 231.

[229]Nicoll, *The Expositor's Greek New Testament,* p. 939.

[230]Morris, *Tyndale New Testament Commentaries,* Vol. 7, p. 233.

Chapter VIII

[231]Acts 24:17; Romans 15:26; 2 Corinthians 8:1 to 9:2.

[232]"God" is not in the Greek text. The subject of the verb is implied. However, this is most clearly parallel with Scripture, for ultimately all blessing comes from God.

[233]2 Corinthians 7:2, 12; Nicoll, *The Expositor's Greek New Testament,* p. 948.

[234]Morris, *Tyndale New Testament Commentaries,* Vol. 7, pp. 247, 248.

[235]Nicoll, *The Expositor's Greek New Testament,* pp. 952, 953.

Bibliography

Buttrick, George A., ed. *The Interpreter's Bible.* New York: Abingdon Press, 1953, Vol. 10.

Clark, J. R. *On the Way to Immortality and Eternal Life.* Salt Lake City, 1950.

Clarke, Adam. *Clarke's Commentary.* New York: Abingdon Press.

Ellicott, Charles. *A Bible Commentary for English Readers.* London: Cassell and Co., n.d., Vol. 7.

Erdman, Charles. *The First Epistle of Paul to the Corinthians.* Philadelphia: Westminster Press, 1966.

Fee, Donald. *Notes on 1 Corinthians.* Kirkland, WA: Northwest College, 1969.

Gee, Donald. *Spiritual Gifts in the Work of the Ministry Today.* Springfield, MO: Gospel Publishing House, 1963.

Grosheide, Frederick W. *Commentary on First Corinthians* (New International Commentary on the New Testament). Grand Rapids: Wm. B. Eerdmans Publishing Co., 1953.

Halley, Henry H. *Halley's Bible Handbook.* Grand Rapids: Zondervan Publishing House, 1965.

Harrison, Everett F., ed. *Baker's Dictionary of Theology.* Grand Rapids: Baker Book House, 1960.

Henry, Matthew. *Commentary on the Whole Bible.* Old Tappan, NJ: Fleming H. Revell, Vol. 6.

Hodges, Melvin. "A Distinct Experience," *Paraclete,* Vol. 6, No. 2, 1972, p. 22.

Hovey, Alvah, ed. *An American Commentary on the New Testament.* Valley Forge, PA: Judson Press, 1887, Vol. 5.

Jamieson, Robert; A. R. Fausset; David Brown. *A Commentary, Critical, Experimental, and Practical on the Old & New Testaments.* Grand Rapids: Wm. B. Eerdmans Publishing Company, 1945, Vol. 6.

Jones, Russell Bradley. *A Survey of the Old and New Testaments.* Grand Rapids: Baker Book House, 1957.

Lenski, Richard C. *The Interpretation of First & Second Corinthians.* Minneapolis: Augsburg Publishing House, 1935.

Luck, G. Coleman. *First Corinthians* (Everyman's Bible Commentary). Chicago: Moody Press, 1967.

Machen, J. Gresham. *New Testament Greek for Beginners.* New York: Macmillan Company, 1951.

Morgan, G. Campbell. *Living Messages of the Books of the Bible.* Old Tappan, NJ: Fleming H. Revell, 1912.

Morris, Leon. *Tyndale New Testament.* Grand Rapids: Wm. B. Eerdmans Publishing Co., 1958, Vol. 7.

Moulton, Harold K. *The Analytical Greek Lexicon Revised.* Grand Rapids: Zondervan Publishing House, rev. ed. 1978.

Nicoll, W. Robertson, ed. *The Expositor's Greek New Testament.* Grand Rapids: Wm. B. Eerdmans Publishing Co., 1952, Vol. 2.

Pearlman, Myer. *Knowing the Doctrines of the Bible.* Springfield, MO: Gospel Publishing House, 1937.

Riggs, Ralph M. *The Spirit Himself.* Springfield, MO: Gospel Publishing House, 1949.

Spence, H. D., and Joseph S. Exell, ed. *The Pulpit Commentary.* Grand Rapids: Wm. B. Eerdmans Publishing Co., 1962, Vol. 19.

Tenney, Merrill C. *New Testament Survey.* Grand Rapids: Wm. B. Eerdmans Publishing Co., rev. ed. 1961.

Thayer, Joseph H. *Greek-English Lexicon of the New Testament.* Grand Rapids: Zondervan Publishing House, 1962.

Thiessen, Henry C. *Lectures in Systematic Theology.* Grand Rapids: Wm. B. Eerdmans Publishing Co., 1949.

Thrall, Margaret E. *First & Second Letters of Paul to the Corinthians* (New English Bible Commentaries). New Rochelle, NY: Cambridge University Press, 1965.

Index

A

Achaicus, 13, 168, 169
Adam, 144, 154-55
Adultery, 50
Agape (church supper), 100-101
  See also: Love
Ambrosiaster, 147
Angels, 48, 96-97, 152, 153
Apollos, 12, 13, 21, 30, 34, 37, 165, 166, 170
Apostles
  appearances of Jesus, 139
  definition, 113
  example, 37-39
  perils of, 149
Aquila, 11, 12, 170
Aquinas, 14

B

Baptism for the dead, 146-148
Baptism in the Holy Spirit, 112
Baptism, Water
  See: water baptism
Barnabas, 14, 77
Beza, Theodore, 147
Body
  See also: Church
  changes in, 153-154
  definition, 52
  destiny, 52
  purpose, 51

resurrection of, 141-143
spiritual vs. natural, 154-157
temple of Holy Spirit, 53
Builders, 31-32

C

Calvin, 147
Carnality, 30
Celibacy, 57, 64-68
Cephas
  See: Peter
Chloe, 13, 21
Chrysostom, 14, 147
Church
  as Body of Christ, 52, 111-113
  as God's possession, 33
  as a unit, 170
Church discipline, 43-46, 48
Circumcision, 62, 80
Clement, 14
Clement of Alexandria, 14
Collection (Offering), 161-163
Conscience, 36, 71, 75, 90, 91
Corinth, 9-11
Corinthian church
  censure, 99
  characteristics, 150, 167-168, 172
  commendation, 94
  description, 14
  divisions, 21, 100
  former state, 106
  immaturity, 29-30

problems, 13, 21
pride, 24, 37, 43, 45, 118
spiritual gifts, 122
wisdom, 86-87
Corinthians, 1
authenticity, 14-15
author, 14, 17
coauthor, 17
date, 12-13
lost letter, 13
occasion of writing, 13
teaching, 15
vocabulary, 14
Covenant, 87, 103
Covetousness, 46, 50
Crispus, 12, 22
Cross, 22, 23-24, 87
"Cup of blessing," 87

D

Death, 34, 143, 146, 157-158, 159
Demons, 88-89, 110
Division, 13, 21, 30, 99-100, 113
Divorce, 58-61
Drunkenness, 47, 50

E

Edification, 72, 89, 118-120, 134
Excommunication, 46-47
Extortion, 46, 50

F

Fellowship
with Christ, 19, 87
with others, 18, 25
Fornication, 43, 46, 49, 51, 53, 85
Fortunatus, 13, 168, 169
Fruit of the Spirit, 107

G

Gaius, 22
Gallio, 12
Games
gladiatorial, 10
Isthmian, 81-82
Gift of discerning of spirits, 110, 129
Gift of faith, 108-109
Gift of governments, 114
Gift of "helps" 113-114
Gift of interpretation of tongues, 111, 128
Gift of knowledge, 108
Gift of prophecy, 109-110, 118, 119, 120, 121, 125-127, 129, 130
Gift of tongues, 106, 110-111, 118, 119, 120-125, 126, 128-129
Gift of wisdom, 107-108
Gift of working of miracles, 109
Gifts of healing, 109
Gifts of the Spirit, 106-107, 114, 119, 127-128, 129-131
Glossolalia
See: Gifts of tongues
God
glory of, 91
grace of, 18, 28
knowledge of, 28
love of, 24
power of, 22
wisdom of, 26, 33
Gospel
advance of, 80
as means of salvation, 137
as revelation of God, 23
as wisdom, 26
mystery of, 26, 27
preached by Paul, 138
Greeks, 23, 141

H

"Heavenly bodies," 152-153

Hermas, 14
Holy Communion
  See: Lord's Supper
Holy Spirit
  manifestations of, 106-111
  work of, 27, 28, 111
Homosexuality, 49-50

I

Idolatry, 47, 50, 72, 84-86, 88-89
Ignatius, 14
Immaturity, 29-30
  See also: Maturity
Incest, 43
Iraneus, 14
Israelites, 83-84

J

James, 139
  Jerusalem church, 161
Jesus Christ
  contrasted with Adam, 154-156
  judge, 36
  kingship, 145-146
  life in, 34, 155
  Lord of Glory, 27
  lordship, 106
  mind of, 29
  office of, 35
  preexistence, 84
  post-resurrection appearances,
    139-140
  resurrection, 137-145, 155
  second coming, 18, 65, 145,
    157-158
  work of, 25, 73, 146
Jews, 23, 80
Judging
  of angels, 48
  of church members, 47
  of sinners, 47
  of stewards, 36

of teachers, 36-37
of the world, 48
worthy of, 48-49
Justice, 48, 49
Justification, 50, 159
Justus (Titus Justus), 11

K

Kingdom of God, 50
Knowledge, 71-73

L

Labor, 76-79
Law, 159
Lawsuits, 47-49
Liberty, 51, 74-75, 89, 91
Lord's Supper, 84, 87-89, 99-105,
  112
Love
  agape, 168
  as character of God, 114
  characteristic of, 116
  guide in conduct, 75, 89
  motivated by 115, 118
  permanence of, 117
  supremacy of, 115, 117-118
  vs. knowledge, 72, 73
Lust, 84
Luther, 131, 147

M

Malice, 46
Man
  as head of woman, 94
  as image of God, 95-96
  hair, 97-98
  natural vs. spiritual, 28-29
  pride of, 33-34
  spirit of, 27, 110
  wisdom of 23, 33

Maranatha, 171-172
Marcionites, 147
Marriage, 55-69
  mixed, 58-59
  normalcy, 55
  obligations & rights, 55-56
  sexual abstinence, 56, 68
Maturity, 30, 72, 75
  See also: Immaturity
Meat
  definition, 75
  sacrificial, 73-74, 89-91
Menander, 150
Ministers, 30-31, 34, 35, 78, 168-169
Mormons, 147
Muratorian Canon, 14
Murmuring, 85
Mystery, 26, 27, 157

Philo, 153
Polycarp, 14
Pride 33, 40-41, 85-86
  See also: Corinthian church
Principle of "abiding," 57-64
Priscilla, 12, 170
Prophets, 113, 120, 130
Prostitutes, 95

R

Railer, 47
Rephidim rock, 83-84
Resurrection, 141-142, 144, 146, 150-152
  See also: Body
  Jesus Christ
Revilement, 50

O

Oecumenius, 14
Offense to others, 91-92
Origen, 14

S

Sadducees, 141
Sanctification, 17, 18, 50
Satan, 44-45, 89
Self-consciousness, 27
Self-examination, 36, 104-105
Self-indulgence, 83
Sin, doctrine of, 159
Slaves, 53, 63, 95
Social morality, 43-69
Sosthenes, 12, 17
Stephanas, 13, 168, 169
Stewardship, 35-36
Sunday observance, 162

P

Paul
  apostleship, 75-76
  appearance of Jesus, 139-140
  as spiritual father, 39-41
  at Corinth, 10, 11-14
  "dying daily," 149
  example, 75, 92
  marital status, 57
  ministry of, 22
  preaching of, 25-26, 34, 79
  purpose, 80, 81
  qualifications of, 17
  renunciation of rights, 78-79
  self-discipline, 81-82
  visit to Corinth 162, 163-164
Peter, 21, 34, 37, 77, 139

T

Teachers, 113, 121
Temptation, 86
Tempting God, 85
Tertullian, 14, 147
Theodoret, 14
Theft, 50
Timothy, 40, 80, 165-166

U

Unity, 21-22, 87, 112
See also: Division

V

Victory, 159-160

W

Water baptism, 22, 111

Wisdom, 26-29
See also: God
Man
Woman
equality, 93, 97
hair, 98
head-covering, 94, 98-99
rights, 56
speaking in church, 131-133
subordination, 93-96, 99
World
attitude toward, 65-66
definition of, 34
spirit of, 28
Worship, Public, 93-135, 162